The
School
Years

Current issues in the
socialization of young people

edited by
JOHN C. COLEMAN

METHUEN

First published in 1979 *by*
Methuen & Co. Ltd
11 *New Fetter Lane, London* EC4P 4EE

Published in the USA by
Methuen & Co.
in association with Methuen, Inc.
733 *Third Avenue, New York, NY* 10017

Printed in Great Britain
at the University Press, Cambridge

British Library Cataloguing in Publication Data

The school years. – (Psychology in progress).
1. Child psychology
2. Adolescent psychology
I. Coleman, John Christopher, b. 1940
II. Series
155.4'24   BF721   79–41114

ISBN 0–416–71190–1
ISBN 0–416–71200–2 Pbk

WITHDRAWN

Psychology

in

Progress

General editor: Peter Herriot

The
School
Years

Psychology in Progress

Contents

Notes on the contributors

John C. Coleman is at present Senior Lecturer in Psychology at the London Hospital Medical College, University of London. His interests cover a wide range of issues within developmental psychology. He is the author of *Relationships in Adolescence* (Routledge and Kegan Paul, 1974) and *The Nature of Adolescence* (Methuen, 1980).

Ronald Davie is Professor of Educational Psychology in the Department of Education, University College Cardiff, where he is principally concerned with postgraduate research and with in-service training for experienced teachers. Before going to Cardiff he was Director of Research at the National Children's Bureau and was closely involved in directing the National Child Development Study for many years. His current research includes an international, collaborative project in the pre-school field and a study of the effects of institutional change in secondary schools upon their children's behaviour problems and learning difficulties.

Elizabeth Douvan is Professor of Psychology and Program Director at the Institute for Social Research, University of Michigan. She has published widely, and is co-author of *The Adolescent Experience* (John Wiley, 1966). Her research interests include adolescent development, family relationships and friendship. She is currently analysing national

(US) data on norms, attitudes and experience in the areas of marriage and parenting.

Rodney Maliphant is Director of the MSc (Educational Psychology) Professional Training Course and Senior Lecturer at University College, London. He was a member of the Home Secretary's Advisory Committee on Juvenile Delinquency, and has worked in both the approved school service and local authority services. His present research interests include recidivism, deprivation, the relationship of autonomic responses to deviancy and the acquisition of reading skills in children.

Phillida Salmon is a clinical psychologist now involved in teaching developmental psychology. She is currently Senior Lecturer in Child Development at the Institute of Education, University of London. Her orientation is broadly that of personal construct theory, and in this area she has published 'A psychology of personal growth' in D. Bannister (ed.) *Perspectives in Personal Construct Theory* (Academic Press, 1970), 'Grids with child subjects' in P. Slater (ed.) *Explorations in Intra-personal Space* (Wiley, 1976), and 'Doing psychological research' in F. Fransella (ed.) *Personal Construct Psychology* (forthcoming).

Helen Weinreich-Haste lectures in psychology at the University of Bath. Her teaching and research interests are in both social and developmental psychology. She has researched and published on the development of moral and social cognition, and has worked on developmental and social aspects of sex roles, including sex role stereotypes and their effects on achievement motivation. She has also done research on the image of science.

Christopher Wilson has worked as a psychologist with maladjusted children, and has also conducted research on conversation, communications media, and reactions to art. He obtained his PhD at the London School of Economics in the field of social psychology and his thesis has been published under the title *Jokes* (Academic Press, 1979).

Editor's introduction

The psychology of human development has until recently contained a noticeable bias. Far more attention has been paid to the first few years than to any of the later stages of the life cycle. The undue emphasis on infancy and early childhood has resulted primarily from the belief that events which occur at the beginning of life form the foundation stones for subsequent development. The model of human growth and change which underlies this belief is as old as history, but was given especial impetus by the Freudian view of man, with its concentration on the significance of infantile sexuality. In general, developmental psychologists have assumed that the earlier the event or experience in a child's life, the more fundamental its contribution to the individual's make-up (see for example, Bloom, 1964). Such a view is closely associated with the concept of irreversibility, referring in particular to the belief that the earlier trauma or deprivation occur the more enduring their effects are likely to be.

In recent years, however, there has been a growing realization of the necessity to correct such a bias. Some, for example, have challenged the view that early, potentially damaging experiences are necessarily irreversible (Clarke and Clarke, 1976). Other writers have acknowledged that events which occur in later stages of development, especially during transitional periods such as adolescence, can have equally profound effects upon the individual. A third important element in this changing climate of opinion is the increasing awareness that psychologists can and should have serious contributions to make where important social questions are concerned. Many of these do not pertain to early childhood. Questions relating to the place of teenagers in society, for example, are questions to which developmental and social psychologists should be addressing themselves, and it is heartening to see that they are being encouraged to do so by bodies such as the Social Science Research Council (Schaffer and Hargreaves, 1978).

The very existence of this book – and the topics covered within it – reflects such a state of affairs. Each chapter addresses itself to an issue which has both theoretical and practical relevance. More than that, however, the subjects chosen for discussion are ones in which major advances have taken place in recent years. Theories of adolescence (Chapter 1) have been fundamentally affected by the availability of empirical data concerning the adolescent experience; the self-concept (Chapter 2) is coming to be seen as a central feature of personality development in the young person, while concepts of morality (Chapter 3) have in the last few years received more attention than almost any other aspect of social maturation. Sex-role learning (Chapter 4) is a topic of great concern to all who are disturbed by the inequalities which still exist in our society, as well as being an issue of immense theoretical interest. The role of the peer group (Chapter 5) could hardly be more topical, for with an apparently increasing trend towards 'age segregation' there is an urgent need for a greater understanding of the part played by the peer group in the socialization process. It is becoming more and more apparent that relations between home and school (Chapter 6) hold the key to the child's intellectual progress, and, finally, delinquency among the young (Chapter 7), as everyone will be aware, represents one of the most pressing social problems of today. Social scientists have significant contributions to make in all these areas. The proof of this assertion will, it is hoped, be found in the following pages.

I would like to express my thanks to Peter Herriot, and to all at Methuen who have provided support in bringing this project to fruition.

JOHN C. COLEMAN

References

Bloom, B. S. (1964) *Stability and Change in Human Characteristics*. New York: John Wiley.

Clarke, A. M. and Clarke, A. D. B. (1976) *Early Experience: Myth and Evidence*. London: Open Books.

Schaffer, H. R. and Hargreaves, D. (1978) Young people in society: an SSRC research initiative. *Bulletin British Psychological Society 31*: 91–4.

1 Current views of the adolescent process

John C. Coleman

Introduction

Two important changes have occurred during the last decade or so in approaches to adolescence. In the first place writers have become much more reluctant to describe these years as a single stage in the life cycle. It is now recognized that adolescence is far from being a static phenomenon, a label as it were, that can be hung around the necks of young people. It makes more sense to view the adolescent years as a dynamic period, involving continual change and transition, for thirteen- and eighteen-year-olds are not easily bracketed together, and there may be as much difference between two fourteen-year-olds as between individuals with five years' difference in chronological age. It is for this reason that adolescence is more likely today to be described as a process rather than a stage.

The second change has come about as a result of an increasing awareness of the contribution of research to our understanding of adolescence. Since the beginning of the 1960s empirical evidence on this topic has become much more widely available, and the results of large-scale studies of young people have gradually been incorporated into the literature. The evidence gained from these studies has, as we shall see in the course of this chapter, forced a drastic re-evaluation of some of the common myths concerning adolescence, thus substantially altering many of the generally accepted views of the condition of young people in our society.

In this chapter I shall attempt to outline the way in which these changes in approach have placed adolescence in a new perspective. In order to do this I shall briefly summarize the two main theoretical viewpoints on adolescence – those of the psychoanalysts and the sociologists – and then go on to evaluate three fundamental concepts deriving from these viewpoints in the light of empirical evidence. The three concepts which I have chosen – 'storm and stress', 'the generation gap' and 'identity crisis' – while not the only concepts relating to adolescence are certainly the ones with the longest history and the ones which have their roots most firmly in the two bodies of theory. In order to examine these roots let us first of all turn to psychoanalysis.

The psychoanalytic approach

Of all the theoretical contributions to the study of adolescence it is probably the psychoanalytic tradition which has had the most powerful impact. To take one of the most well-known contributors, Anna Freud, in her book *The Ego and the Mechanisms of Defence* (1937), elaborated her father's early theories of psychosexual development by stressing the role of the psychological defence mechanisms in determining behaviour. In her view, and in that of most psychoanalysts, the psychological defences developed in childhood are not sufficient to deal with the upsurge of instincts which occurs as a result of puberty. This increase in instinctual life upsets the psychic balance, and leads, so it is argued, to a state of internal emotional upheaval, which is in turn reflected in overt behaviour.

Of the present-day writers who have developed and elaborated on such views, one of the most worthwhile is Peter Blos (1962; 1967). In his opinion adolescence may be conceptualized as a 'second individuation process', the first having been completed towards the end of the third year of life. Blos argues that both periods have a number of features in common. In both there is an increased vulnerability in the organization of the personality, in both there is an urgent need for psychological change to meet the major maturational movements, and finally both periods are followed by specific psychopathology should development go awry. What is in infancy a 'hatching from the symbiotic membrane to become an individual toddler' (Mahler, 1963) becomes in adolescence the renunciation of dependency on the family and the loosening of the early childhood ties which have, until puberty, been the major source of emotional nurturance. It is this notion of disengagement which opens the way for the finding of love objects outside the family. In some senses just the reverse has happened in early childhood. Here, the child, in an attempt to become separate from the loved one, namely the mother, internalizes her. This allows him to become independent while retaining inside himself a representation of the figure he needs. In adolescence just the opposite must occur – in order to gain independence the individual has to give up the internalized infantile object in order to seek new love objects in the outside world.

If for the psychoanalysts disengagement is one essential feature of adolescence, another feature of equal importance is regression. By this is usually meant a manifestation of behaviour more appropriate to earlier stages of development. Blos provides a number of examples of such behaviour. One that he chooses is the adolescent's idolization of famous people, especially pop stars and celebrated sportsmen and sportswomen. In this phenomenon, he argues, we are reminded of the idealized parent of the younger child. Another example of behaviour in which can be recognized reflections of earlier states is the emotional condition similar to 'merger'. By this is meant the sensation on the part of one individual of becoming totally submerged by or 'at one' with another individual. In this condition the adolescent might become almost completely absorbed in abstract ideas such as Nature or Beauty, or with political, religious or philosophical ideals. These states, especially those which are drug induced, are sought as a temporary refuge, and they act, Blos argues, as safeguards against total merger with the early idealized parent figure.

Further examples which Blos provides serve to illustrate the way in which the process of disengagement leads to regressive behaviour. One such example is the adolescent's need for group experiences, or individual relationships and sensations which provide vivid and acute excitement. Blos feels that the frequent and abrupt changes so often seen in these relationships are indications of their essential shallowness, and what appears to be the motive force behind them is not the need for personal contact but the intensity of feeling and agitation of emotions which they provide. He places firmly in this category the need to do things 'just for kicks' which, he argues, is a way of escaping loneliness, boredom and dullness. He also includes here the search for drug and mystical experiences. To describe this condition, Blos uses the term 'affect and object hunger', and he suggests that the adolescent need for intense emotional states may be seen as a means of coping with the inner emptiness which follows the breaking of the childhood ties. Blos goes on to indicate his belief that both object and affect hunger find some relief in the adolescent gang or peer group. This social group is often, quite literally, the substitute for the adolescent's family, and within it he may experience all the feelings so essential for individual growth, such as stimulation, empathy, belong-ingness, the opportunity for role playing, identification, and the sharing of guilt and anxiety.

In the process of disengagement from early childhood figures who are both loved and hated, one other throwback to earlier modes of behaviour is very much in evidence, and this is ambivalence. From this stems much of the aggression, the negativism, the indifference and the plainly obstructive behaviour. As seen by Blos, ambivalence accounts for many of the phenomena often considered incomprehensible in adolescent behaviour. The emotional instability of relationships, and the contradictions in thought and feeling reflect the fluctuations be-tween loving and hating, active and passive, involvement and non-involvement which underlie relationships in the early years of life, and which are reactivated in extreme form in adolescence. Nonconformity is an almost universal feature of adolescent behaviour, and Blos believes that, in a sense, it is one of the most adaptive defences against the regressive pull. To illustrate this, he quotes an especially articulate insightful adolescent girl (1967, p. 178):

> If you act in opposition to what is expected, you bump right and left into regulations and rules. Today when I ignored school – just didn't go – it made me feel very good. It gave me a sense of being a person, not just an automaton. If you continue to rebel and bump into the world around you often enough, then an outline of yourself gets drawn in your mind. You need that. Maybe, when you know who you are, you don't have to be different from those who know, or think they know who you should be.

In summary, what exactly is the 'individuation' which Blos sees as the principal component of adolescent development? It appears that for him this process involves the growing person in taking increasing responsibility for what he is and for what he does, rather than depositing this responsibility on the shoulders of the parents. However, the process of individuation can only be successfully achieved as a result of disengagement from early childhood attachments. These attachments, though, can only be surrendered, according to the psychoanalysts, by a re-animation of infantile involvements and patterns of behaviour. As Blos puts it: 'The adolescent has to come into emotional contact with the passions of his infancy and early childhood, in order for them to surrender their original cathexes; only then can the past fade into conscious and unconscious memories ...' (1967, p. 178). By 'cathexis' is meant emotional force or impact. The French have a phrase: 'reculer pour mieux sauter', which roughly means: to retreat first in order to leap further. This seems to describe the process succinctly.

Thus it can be seen that the achievement of 'second individuation' hinges on regression. In a paradoxical fashion progress is precluded unless earlier forms of behaviour are allowed expression. In Blos's view, adolescence is the only period in human development during which regression is an obligatory component of normal maturation. He believes that this 'normal' and 'necessary' regression inevitably causes much transient maladaptive behaviour, and explains many of the easily recognized features of adolescent behaviour such as emotional turbulence, ambivalence, rebelliousness, negativism and so on. The value, therefore, of psychoanalytic ideas in general and Blos's writings in particular may be seen to lie firstly in the provision of plausible explanations for much seemingly puzzling behaviour, and secondly because they illustrate clearly the firm foundations in which are embedded fundamental concepts such as 'storm and stress'.

While Blos's position within psychoanalytic theory is an important one, no discussion of the psychoanalytic viewpoint would be complete without some mention of Erik Erikson. Readers will probably be familiar with his belief that the major developmental task for the adolescent is the establishment of identity and the defeat of identity diffusion. These ideas are most easily accessible in his books *Childhood and Society* (1963) and *Identity: Youth and Crisis* (1968). One of the problems with Erikson, however, is that he is not an easy writer to pin down. He rarely makes definitive statements, preferring, as he says himself, to let concepts define themselves by 'use and allusion'. In general, however, he appears to believe that the search for identity becomes especially acute during adolescence as a result of rapid change in the biological, social and psychological spheres of life, and because of the necessity for occupational decisions to be made, ideals to be accepted or rejected, and sexual and friendship choices to be determined. Unfortunately, he has made little effort to be specific about the range of individual variation to be expected, and his use of terms such as 'normative crisis' and 'the psychopathology of everyday adolescence' has led to the assumption that in his view some form of stress, turmoil or disturbance of identity is to be anticipated in most young people, particularly during the stage of late adolescence.

In order to understand fully Erikson's point of view, one further step in his thinking needs to be mentioned: this involves the notion of adolescence as a period of *psychosocial moratorium*. Just as, in psychoanalytic theory, the latency stage may be viewed as a time of psychosexual delay, a time when in a sense sexual development is in abeyance, so, argues Erikson, a similar situation applies in adolescence, only with regard to identity. In his view society allows, or even creates, a time of life when the individual may delay major identity decisions, when he may experiment with roles in order that he may discover what sort of a person he is and is not. It could be argued that it is precisely for this reason that there is a crisis at all. The opportunity and even pressure to experiment freely combined with a vulnerability of personality structure are obvious causal factors which may underlie crises in development. Erikson expresses it clearly when he writes:

> It is true, of course, that the adolescent, during the final stage of his identity formation, is apt to suffer more deeply than he ever did before or ever will again from a confusion of roles. And it is also true that such confusion renders many an adolescent defenceless against the sudden impact of previously latent malignant disturbances. But it is important to emphasize that the diffused and vulnerable, aloof and uncommitted, yet demanding and opinionated personality of the not too neurotic adolescent contains many necessary elements of a semi-deliberate role experimentation of the 'I dare you' and 'I dare myself' variety. Much of this apparent confusion thus must be considered social play – the true genetic successor of childhood play. Similarly, the adolescent's ego development demands and permits playful if daring, experimentation in fantasy and introspection. (1968, pp. 163–4)

Through his discussions of self and identity, as well as his concern with roles and role behaviour, Erikson represents a bridge between the psychoanalytic and sociological traditions. His strong belief in inner turbulence as an integral feature of adolescent development is consistent with his psychoanalytic background, but it could be said that he sees further than this, for he is also concerned with the social context of the growing adolescent. Although, as we shall see, his ideas about 'identity crisis' have not been sustained by empirical investigation, he cannot but be admired for his breadth of vision, and almost paradoxically he provides an excellent introduction to the sociological viewpoint.

The sociological approach

There are, it would appear, three distinguishing features which mark the sociological approach to adolescence. These are a concentration on roles, an interest in the development of the self, and a concern with the process of socialization. Needless to say all three are closely interrelated, as is illustrated in Elder's (1968) review of the literature in this area. As Elder points out, it is the belief of most sociologists that a large proportion of an individual's life is characterized by role engagement, and by the building of a role repertoire which constitutes a crucial facet of the self. The years between childhood and adulthood, as a period of emerging identity, are seen as particularly relevant to the construction of this role repertoire, for the following reasons. Firstly, features of adolescence such as growing independence from authority figures, involvement with peer groups, and an unusual sensitivity to the evaluations of others all provoke role transitions and discontinuity, varying in their intensity of course, as a function of both social and cultural context. Secondly, any inner change or uncertainty has the effect of increasing the individual's dependence on others, and this applies particularly to the need for reassurance and support for one's view of oneself. Thirdly, the effects of major environmental changes are also relevant in this context. Different schools, the move from school to university or college, leaving home, taking a job, all demand involvement in a new set of relationships, which in turn lead to different and often greater expectations, a substantial reassessment of the self, and an acceleration of the process of socialization.

In discussing adolescence as a transitional period of personality development Elder himself (1968) takes the theory a step further by distinguishing two types of role change or role discontinuity. On the one hand the adolescent experiences *intra-role change*. In this the individual is exposed to new role demands, since as he gets older expectations gradually increase. His role remains the same, but within that role different things are expected of him – his teacher may expect better performance, his parents more independence, and so on. On the other hand, the individual also acquires entirely *new roles*. Evidently this discontinuity is more abrupt, and is often more difficult to cope with. The change, for example, from school to full-time work, usually requires very considerable adaptation, and remnants of the dependent student role are often seen in the young worker. The acquisition of new roles is usually coupled with gradual changes of an intra-role nature, and the two facilitate or hinder each other depending on factors such as the part played by the parents or other significant figures, the relevance of past learning and skills to new role demands, the range of the adolescent's role repertoire, and so on. In general it is argued that the adolescent experiences more or less discontinuity, and that as the degree of role discontinuity increases, successful adaptation to the new set of role demands becomes more problematic.

Self-image is another factor which is often seen as being closely related to role development, and a number of writers have contributed significantly to theory by considering this aspect of adolescent personality. For example, Rosenberg writes: 'At this stage of development – between about 15 and 18 years of age – the individual tends to be keenly concerned with his self-image. What am I like? How good am I? What should, or might I become? On what basis shall I judge myself? Many adolescents are consumed with questions of this sort' (1965, p. 3).

Rosenberg suggests three reasons for this phenomenon of heightened self-awareness and concern with self-image. Firstly, adolescence is a time of such major change, both physical and psychological, that faced with pressures of this kind any individual would be forced to re-assess and take stock of himself. Secondly, adolescence, particularly late adolescence, is an age at which many fundamental decisions present themselves. It is at this time that the initial occupational decision is usually taken, and also critical sexual choices are often made between the years of seventeen and twenty. As Rosenberg says, when a major factor in these decisions is the individual's view of what sort of person he is, it is not surprising that the self-image comes to the foreground. Finally, adolescence is marked by particular status ambiguity. Society has no clearly defined expectations of the individual during his adolescent years, and therefore responds to him in a manner which must appear ambiguous – at times demanding child-like obedience, and at others expecting the self-confidence and independence of an adult. Rosenberg argues that it is just this sort of ambivalence in others which brings into question the adolescent's own self-image.

There are two other writers who may be mentioned as having contributed to an understanding of the importance of roles in adolescent development. Orville Brim (1965) was particularly interested in the adolescent's views of the prescriptions or expectations that adults hold concerning the behaviour of young people. He argued that the more we know of these perceptions the more we are likely to understand the roles that adolescents adopt. As he puts it:

> We should attempt to describe personality by reference to the individual's perceptions of himself and his behaviour, and of the social organization in which he lives. We should be interested in the kinds of people he says are of the greatest significance to him, and interested in what he thinks others expect him to do, and in what they think about his performances. We should also know whether or not he accepts what others prescribe for him as right and legitimate, or whether he thinks their expectations are unfair.... (1965, p. 156)

In Brim's view, then, the development of role behaviour will be determined to a large extent by an interaction between the individual's relationships with significant others and his or her perceptions of the expectations of those significant figures. Such an argument accords closely with that of Baumrind (1975). In her discussion of adolescent socialization she introduces the concept of *reciprocal role assumption*. By this is meant the effects which prior role assumptions by other family members have on the role the individual may assume. An example which she gives is a situation in which both parents are exceptionally competent managers, thus preventing the young person from developing managerial skills since, while readily available for modelling, such skills are not needed within the family setting. Another example might be a mother who assumes a child-like dependent role, thus forcing her daughter into a maternal role because of the void which she, the mother, creates.

It will be apparent that the point being made by both Brim and Baumrind is that the individual's role behaviour can only be understood within a social context, and that the forces within the environment need to be taken into account in making sense of adolescent development. Elder's (1975) recent discussion of socialization elaborates this theme in some important respects. He makes the point that socialization processes interact with social change, and in particular change which affects the institution of the family. In this respect Elder draws attention to two major social changes which have occurred in recent years: the prolonged dependence of young people as a result of increased opportunities for secondary and higher education, and the decline in the role of the family. According to the sociologists these phenomena have had a number of consequences. In the first place industrialized societies have witnessed increasing age segregation, with a decline in the time adults and teenagers spend together; secondly, the peer group has assumed an ever more important role, precisely as a result of the abdication of responsibility by parents in the upbringing of their teenage children; finally, the adolescent is exposed to a large variety of socialization agencies (secondary school, the peer group, adult-directed youth organizations, the mass media, political organizations and so on) which present him with a wide range of potential conflicts in values and ideals.

All these factors are seen by Elder as making socialization more uncertain, and causing major difficulty for the young person in establishing a bridge towards the assumption of adult roles. Bronfenbrenner (1974), in his discussion of the alienation of young people, has made very similar points, and it appears a common assumption among those working from the sociological point of view that the social changes of the last twenty years or so have created ever increasing stresses for young people. In particular it should be noted that most writers see little of value in what they believe to be the decline of adult involvement and the increasing importance of the peer group. Among such writers the adolescent peer group is frequently described as being more likely to encourage anti-social behaviour than to act as a civilizing agent, and though it is accepted that the effects of peer involvement depend on the standards and activities of the peer group, there is undoubtedly a general feeling that when young people spend a considerable amount of time with individuals of their own age more harm than good is likely to come of it.

While on the one hand there is clearly some logic in the view that the adolescent who is deprived of adult company is at a disadvantage in the transition towards maturity, on the other hand research does not bear out the myth of the all-powerful peer group, as the author's own review indicates (Coleman, 1979). The place of the peer group is a theme dealt with in greater detail in Chapter 5, so that it is not necessary to evaluate it further here. Suffice it to say that the power of the peer group during adolescence is a notion which manifestly has roots in both the sociological and psychoanalytic traditions.

The aim of this chapter is, as has been stated, to review briefly two major approaches to adolescence, in order to illustrate the origins or genealogy of the three concepts which have been chosen for discussion. We have seen how each of the concepts – 'storm and stress', 'the generation gap' and 'identity crisis' – has been given substance by the theoretical views which we have examined. It is these concepts which have, to a large extent, determined everyday notions of adolescence, and thus it is of primary importance to consider how such concepts stand in the light of empirical evidence. Do the results of the large-scale studies of adolescence strengthen or weaken these concepts? It is to this question that we now turn.

Storm and stress

As it happens the phrase 'storm and stress' has a very long history as a description of adolescence, stretching back far further than the psycho-analytic and sociological traditions we have been discussing. Plato and other Greek writers held a view of youth which included the notion of marked emotional upheaval, and the idea of inner turmoil following the years of puberty has been strongly championed by writers down the ages long before the beginning of this century. The first hint that experimental evidence might not entirely corroborate this view of the difficulties of youth came from a study carried out by Westley and Elkin (1957), who worked with a small middle-class sample in Montreal, Canada. They were surprised to find that these teenagers reported remarkably few 'crises', and on the whole described their adolescence as being relatively peaceful and tension-free. This evidence was greeted at first with scepticism, and the investigators were criticized for having used a selected sample consisting primarily of privileged or over-protected young people. However, findings from other larger studies, such as those of Douvan and Adelson (1966), Bandura (1972) and the Offers (Offer, 1969; Offer and Offer, 1975) have all corroborated this picture. Here is how Daniel Offer summarizes his evidence on adolescent turmoil:

The transitional period of adolescence does present the adolescent with a special burden, a challenge, and an opportunity. He has to individualize, build up confidence in himself and his abilities, make important decisions concerning his future, and free himself of his earlier attachments to his parents. Our observations have led us to conclude that the majority of the teenagers in our sample coped with these tasks successfully. They lack the turmoil of the disturbed adolescent precisely because their ego is strong enough to withstand the pressures. . . . It seems to us that someone might eventually raise an objection concerning our subjects that, because of their low level of turmoil, they are cases of arrested development. Certain investigators who have also observed the low level of turmoil in a large number of adolescents have interpreted their findings somewhat differently than we have. . . . Implicitly these investigators have adopted the position that lack of turmoil is a bad prognostic sign and must necessarily prevent the adolescent from developing into a mature adult. All out data, including the psychological testing, point in the opposite direction. The adolescents not only adjusted well; they were also in touch with their feelings and developed meaningful relationships with significant others. (1969, p. 184)

One of the best studies in this area is that which was carried out by Rutter and his colleagues on the Isle of Wight (Rutter et al., 1976). The design of this research had two particular strengths; in the first place it was not only the teenagers who were interviewed, but evidence was also sought both from parents and from teachers, thus providing data from three separate sources; second, the study was distinguished by a rigorous approach to the definition of terms such as 'turmoil' and 'crisis'. The results of this study which are relevant to the concept of 'storm and stress' were as follows. (1) That where psychiatric disorder was concerned there was hardly any difference between ten-year-olds, fourteen-year-olds and adults in the numbers experiencing such disorders. Among females, for example, 10·9 per cent of ten-year-olds, 12·5 per cent of fourteen-year-olds and 11·9 per cent of adults on the Isle of Wight were reported to be experiencing psychiatric difficulties. (2) That a substantial proportion of those who did experience these difficulties during adolescence had problems which had been manifest since childhood. (3) However, where psychiatric problems did first become apparent in adolescence, these were highly likely to be associated with stressful factors in the environment, such as parents' marital difficulties. (4) That among teenagers only approximately 20 per cent agreed with the statement on the self-report inventory: 'I often feel miserable or depressed.'

It will be apparent that predictions which might be derived from a notion of adolescent turmoil hardly accord with these findings. Had this concept any validity one would have been more likely to expect the following: an increased rate of psychiatric disorder among adolescents, a high proportion of newly arising difficulties among young people, many examples of problems where the primary cause was the adolescent experience *per se*, and finally a high proportion of adolescents reporting depression or misery. Rutter's study provides no evidence to support any of these contentions, thus corroborating the results of the American studies and seemingly casting serious doubt on the concept of 'storm and stress'. Naturally, the situation is not as simple as this, and there are a number of possible explanations for the apparent discrepancy between theory and research. It will, however, be more appropriate to consider some of these explanations once we have looked more closely at the two other popular concepts.

The generation gap

According to Bengston (1970) the concept of a 'generation gap' has at least as long a history as that of 'storm and stress'. Thus the first document on ethics of which there is record, that of Ptahhotep the Egyptian sage, was concerned with the problem of the generations, while Plato and Aristotle both incorporated generational struggle in their theories of political change. In fact Aristotle suggested quite explicitly that the cause of political struggle could be found in the conflict of fathers and sons. Similar themes have occurred throughout recorded history, so it is hardly surprising that present day theorists have accorded such notions a prominent place. Once again, however, the tenor of the research evidence does not appear to provide any justification for the wide acceptance of such a concept.

To take one example, Bandura (1972) shows that the idea of the existence of a stressful period of relationships between adults and young people is seriously exaggerated. He takes a number of propositions which stem from the concept of a generation gap, and compares them with his own research findings. Firstly, it is supposed that adolescents are involved in a fundamental struggle to emancipate themselves from parental ties, but Bandura from his research evidence could find no support for this point of view. In his estimation the establishment of independence from parents has been more or less completed by the time the child is thirteen or fourteen, rather than just beginning at this time. In his sample the autonomy of the adolescent seemed to pose more of a problem for the adults than for the teenagers: many parents, for example, regretting the companionship they had lost. Secondly, it is often believed that during adolescence parents become more controlling and restrictive. However, exactly the opposite picture emerged from the interview data, with both adults and youngsters describing how, as the latter moved through adolescence, their relationships became easier and they became more able to trust each other. Finally, Bandura considered conformity to peer group values, and here again found little evidence to support the traditional view. The adolescents whom he interviewed appeared to be discriminating and selective in their choice of reference groups, and there were few signs of 'slavish conformity'. In general, peer group values did not appear to be in direct opposition to family values, nor did it appear that membership of a peer group generated family conflict. As Offer and Offer (1975) expressed it:

> Continuity of values can be seen both between individual parents and their sons and between the parent generation and the adolescent and young adult generation. Peer group values do have an influence on behaviour, but most often the influence can be negated by the stronger inculcated parental values. This conflict, however, seems to be minimal as peer group values themselves are likely to be extensions of parental values. . . . In most instances the teenager or young adult will feel more comfortable within the peer grouping that adopts values similar to his own. (p. 190)

In the field of attitudes there is much recent work to support this point of view. Gustafson (1972) studied over a thousand Scandinavian students, and found that the majority espoused the conventional values of their communities. Most had faith in their parents, and conflicts with the older generation were usually absent. A pleasant home life, including marriage and sexual satisfaction, was very high on their list of important aspirations. Bengston (1970) quotes studies which show that in both political and sexual spheres parents and their teenage children have similar rather than divergent attitudes on important issues. He also notes the surprising fact that all studies have shown there to be a greater agreement over fundamental values between adolescents and their parents than between parents and grandparents. Jennings and Niemi (1975), in their study of political orientation, have made an important contribution in this area by attempting to separate generational differences from secular trends which affect both age groups equally. Their findings show that, if comparisons are made between 1965 and 1973, then the overall impression is of the generations moving closer together, rather than pulling apart. This study is to be especially welcomed in that it underlines the importance of making the distinction between historical changes in attitude which take place in society as a whole and attitude change which occurs simply as a result of growing up. This is an issue which is also stressed in the work of Nesselroade and Baltes (1974).

Another study reporting similar findings is that of Douvan and Adelson (1966). Where morality, political or religious beliefs, or sexual attitudes were concerned adolescents appeared to be largely in agreement with their parents and, far from despising or rejecting their views, seemed to look up to adults and to value their advice. What did emerge from this study, however, was a pattern of minor conflicts between parent and teenager, focussing especially on issues such as makeup, dating, leisure activities, music and so on. A similar picture emerged from a study by Coleman, George and Holt (1977), where again conflicts between the generations centred around dimensions of behaviour such as noisiness, tidiness, and punctuality – reflecting mundane day-to-day issues of living under the same roof – rather than the more fundamental personality dimensions of honesty, perseverance and concern for others. Finally, in this context the work of Rutter et al. (1976) may be mentioned once more. We have already noted his findings that psychiatric difficulties were relatively rare among the Isle of Wight sample. The study also examined the degree of alienation between the generations, as experienced either by the adolescents or by their parents. The results showed that in only 4 per cent of the total group did the parents feel an increase in alienation during adolescence, whilst among the young people themselves only about 5 per cent reported actual rejection of their parents. A further 25 per cent expressed some small degree of criticism. These figures are very much in line with American studies, and all provide support for the view expressed by Adelson when he wrote an article for the *New York Times* in 1970 entitled 'What generation gap?'

Identity crisis

While, as we have seen, concern over the issue of identity is apparent in the sociological approach to adolescence, it is undoubtedly Erikson who has done most to popularize the concept of identity crisis, and it is he more than any other writer who has been responsible for the fact that the term has passed into common usage. As has already been mentioned Erikson is far from being an easy writer to summarize, but is would appear that, for him, there are at least four dimensions of identity crisis (Erikson, 1968):

(1) The problem of intimacy – wanting but not being able to get close to and form mature relationships with an appropriate partner.
(2) Diffusion of time perspective – the difficulty of planning realistically for the future.
(3) Diffusion of industry – an inability to concentrate on the task at hand or a preoccupation with one, usually irrelevant activity.
(4) The choice of a negative identity – often expressed in hostility and rejection towards the roles and identity suggested as proper and desirable.

While dimensions such as these may be familiar and useful in a clinical setting, they have proved exceedingly difficult to translate into empirically meaningful terms. Thus it is clear from an examination of the literature – and here we may include such studies as those of Bronson (1959) and Howard (1960) as well as those of Simmons et al. (1973) – that investigators have in reality seen little difference between concepts of the self and concepts of identity, and thus we may with confidence consider these as one and the same.

In evaluating the evidence on this subject the first important point to make is that, contrary to theoretical expectations, adolescence as a stage in the life cycle does not, in and of itself, necessarily bring with it a change in self-image. Simply because the individual is passing through the teenage years does not alone imply an instability in self-concept. In one of the best studies in this area Engel (1959) was able to demonstrate this clearly. She used a Q-sort technique for the assessment of self-image, and administered the test to boys and girls of 13 and 15, and then again two years later when the subjects were 15 and 17. The results showed a relative stability of self-concept between 13 and 15 as well as between 15 and 17, which was demonstrated by an overall correlation of 0·53 between first and second testing. This correlation compares with a test re-test reliability over ten days of 0·68. However, Engel also showed that those 20 per cent of the sample manifesting a negative self-concept were significantly less stable in their self-image than those in the other group. This is a point to which we shall return later. On the general issue of stability of self-image, it is a great pity that no other longitudinal studies have been carried out. However evidence from both Tomé (1972) and Monge (1973) provide support for the notion of stability of self-image. Both studies, although cross-sectional, investigated the structure of the self-concept at different ages during adolescence, and in the light of their results both writers argue against any major change or reorganization of the self-concept during the years 12 to 18.

Findings which are complementary to this conclusion may be derived from studies which have investigated the development of self-esteem or self-image. On the whole such research has pointed to the conclusion that, again contrary to theoretical expectation, if there is a period in the life cycle when there is lowered self-esteem or increased self-image disturbance this is most likely to be in the pre-adolescent stage rather than during adolescence itself. Thus Piers and Harris (1964), investigating the level of self-esteem in nine-, twelve- and sixteen-year-olds, were able to show that while nine- and sixteen-year-olds had similar levels of self-esteem, in the twelve-year-old group there was a significantly lower level of self-esteem than in the other two groups. This finding is corroborated by the later study of Simmons et al. (1973), referred to earlier in this section. These workers studied various aspects of self-image disturbance in 2,600 children and adolescents between the ages of 8 and 18. They showed, firstly, that it was during the years 11 to 13 that there was the greatest increase in self-consciousness, in instability of self-concepts, and in unfavourable content of the self-image. These dimensions increased greatly during the period around puberty, but thereafter remained at a relatively constant level. Secondly, where self-esteem was concerned the results could not have been more clear. The instance of low self-esteem increased steadily from 8 onwards, reached a peak at 12, and from that time fell sharply.

It is, however, important to point out that although the majority of adolescents may be stable in their self-image and have reasonable or even high self-esteem, there are clearly going to be a minority of whom this is not true. In Engel's study, as has been mentioned, some 20 per cent had a negative self-image on first testing and this group had the greatest level of instability of self-image over the two year period. In addition, those with a negative self-image also had higher maladjustment scores on various personality tests. Such findings are consistent with other work in the area. Thus Rosenberg (1965) showed that between 20 and 30 per cent of his sample could be classified as having low self-esteem, and in the author's own work (Coleman, 1974) in which four age groups were compared, approximately 30 per cent of the sample expressed negative responses on a sentence-completion test relating to self-image. Thus it seems probable that a small minority of post-pubertal adolescents are likely to present themselves at clinics or consultation centres because of disturbance or disorientation of self-concept. What is quite clear, however, from the experimental evidence is that the classical concept of 'identity crisis' simply does not apply to the large majority of adolescents in the general population.

Reconciling the contradictions

Our review up to this point has indicated that, while all three common concepts are firmly rooted in theoretical traditions, none of them are supported by the research evidence. Thus there is, in a sense, an apparent division between what might be called the 'classical' and the 'empirical' points of view. We must now consider whether such differences can be reconciled.

In exploring this question it must first of all be stated that there are a number of obvious reasons which could underlie the differences of opinion between the two schools of thought. In the first place, as many writers have pointed out, psychoanalysts and psychiatrists see a selected population. Their experience of adolescence is based on what they see in clinics and hospitals, and this must create a one-sided view of the teenage years, a view which is likely to include an over-representation of problems of adjustment. Secondly, certain aspects of adolescent behaviour, such as vandalism, delinquency, drug-taking and sexual promiscuity are extremely threatening to adults, and the few who are involved in these activities attain undue prominence in the public eye. The mass media, in their search for sensationalism, are eager to publicize behaviour of this sort, and it is only too easy to understand how for many adults the minority comes to be representative of all adolescents. There is a third possible reason for the divergence of view, which is that the psychologists responsible for large-scale surveys have tended to over-estimate the individual adolescent's ability or willingness to talk about his innermost feelings. Much depends on the way the study is carried out, but it is important to remember how very difficult it is for anyone, let alone an anxious or resentful teenager, to share fears, worries or conflicts with a strange interviewer. While the first two reasons may have led the proponents of the 'classical' view to exaggerate the universality of, say, the 'generation gap', it may also be true that the third reason has led those responsible for the 'empirical' view to under-estimate to some degree the amount of inner stress which can be experienced by young people at some periods of their adolescence.

It seems most probable that the truth of the matter lies somewhere in between the two opposing viewpoints. Adolescence can be a time of serious disturbance and disruption, but only for the few, and then usually at only one period during the adolescent years. The majority of young people, during most of the stages of adolescence, get on well with adults, cope with the demands of school or job, contribute to society, and achieve major adjustments with only minimal signs of stress. How do they do it? It is this contradiction, between the amount of overall change experienced, and the relative health and resilience of the individuals involved in such change, which now requires some consideration.

In an earlier paper (Coleman, 1978) I outlined a 'focal' theory of adolescence, in the hope that this would go some way towards resolving such a contradiction. However, before this is explained it will be necessary briefly to outline the background of this 'focal' theory. The theory grew out of the results of a study of normal adolescents (Coleman, 1974). Large groups of boys and girls at the ages of 11, 13, 15 and 17 were given a set of identical tests which elicited from them attitudes and opinions about a wide range of relationships. Thus material was included on self-image, being alone, heterosexual relationships, parental relationships, friendships and large group situations. The material was analysed in terms of the constructive and negative elements present in these relationship situations, and in terms of the common themes expressed by the young people involved in the study. Findings showed that attitudes to all relationships changed as a function of age, but more importantly the results also indicated that concern about different issues reached a peak at different stages in the adolescent process. This finding is illustrated for boys in Figure 1.1, where it can be seen that simply by considering three of the most prominent themes, there are peak ages for the expression of each of these various concerns. Similar results are obtained for girls.

It was this finding that led to the formulation of a focal theory. The theory proposes that at different ages particular sorts of relationship

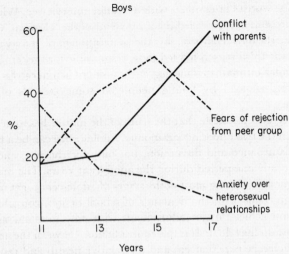

Boys

Fig. 1.1   Peak ages for the expression of different themes. Data derived from Coleman (1974).

patterns come into focus, in the sense of being most prominent, but that no pattern is specific to one age only. Thus the patterns overlap, different issues come into focus at different times, but simply because an issue is not the most prominent feature of an age, this does not mean that it may not be critical for some individuals. These ideas, combined with empirical findings such as those illustrated in Figure 1.1 above, combine to suggest a symbolic model of adolescent development, where each curve represents a different issue or relationship. This is portrayed in Figure 1.2.

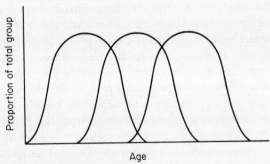

Fig. 1.2   Focal models. Each curve represents a different issue or relationship. After Coleman (1974).

In many ways such a notion is not dissimilar from any traditional stage theory. However, it carries with it a very much more flexible view of development, and therefore differs from stage theory in three important respects. In the first place the resolution of one issue is not seen as the *sine qua non* for tackling the next. In fact it is clearly envisaged that a minority of individuals will find themselves facing more than one issue at the same time. Secondly, the theory does not assume the existence of fixed boundaries between stages, and therefore issues are not necessarily linked with a particular age or development level. Finally, there is nothing immutable about the sequence involved. In our culture it appears that individuals are more likely to face certain issues in the early stages of adolescence, and different issues at other stages, but the 'focal' theory is not dependent on a fixed sequence, and it would be of very great interest to examine other cultures in the light of this theory of development.

It is the author's belief that the 'focal' theory of adolescent development may provide a clue to the resolution of the apparent contradiction between the amount of disruption implicit in adolescence on the one hand, and the relatively successful adaptation among the general population on the other. If adolescents have to adjust to so much potentially stressful change, and at the same time pass through this stage of their life with relative stability, as the 'empirical' view indicates, how do they do it? The answer which is suggested by the 'focal' theory is that they cope by dealing with one issue at a time. They spread the process of adaptation over a span of years, attempting to resolve first one issue, and then the next. Different problems, different relationship issues come into focus and are tackled at different stages, so that the stresses resulting from the need to adapt to new modes of behaviour are rarely concentrated all at one time. It follows from this that it is precisely in those who, for whatever reason, do have more than one issue to cope with at a time that problems are most likely to occur. Thus, for example, where puberty and the growth spurt occur at the normal time individuals are able to adjust to these changes before other pressures, such as those from parents and teachers, are brought to bear. For the later maturers, however, pressures are more likely to occur simultaneously, inevitably requiring adjustments over a much wider area.

The 'focal' theory is only one of a number of possible ways of conceptualizing adolescent development. It has the particular advantage, however, of being based on empirical evidence, and in a sense it could be said that this chapter has been concerned as much as anything with the effects of empirical evidence on traditional theories of adolescence. Studies over the past few years have made a very considerable dent in the common concepts which we have been examining, and what is now urgently needed is a new theoretical approach which incorporates not only the empirical evidence but also an awareness of the dynamic and changing nature of adolescence. It will be recalled that it was with these two issues that we began the chapter. It was pointed out that current views of the teenage years are being affected first by a realization that adolescence is not a stage but a process, and second by the availability of evidence from large-scale research studies. It is these two important factors which must be taken into account if theories of adolescence are to remain up to date, and it is to be hoped that the suggestion of a 'focal' theory will at least stimulate others to give careful thought to the plausibility of both 'classical' and 'empirical' approaches to adolescence.

References

Adelson, J. (1970) What generation gap? *New York Times Magazine*, 18 Jan., pp. 10ff.

Bandura, A. (1972) The stormy decade: fact or fiction? In D. Rogers (ed.) *Issues in Adolescent Psychology* (2nd edition). New York: Appleton-Century–Crofts.

Baumrind, D. (1975) Early socialization and adolescent competence. In S. E. Dragastin and G. Elder (eds) *Adolescence in the Life Cycle*. New York: John Wiley.

Bengston, V. L. (1970) The generation gap. *Youth and Society 2*: 7–32.

Blos, P. (1962) *On Adolescence*. London: Collier-Macmillan.

Blos, P. (1967) The second individuation process of adolescence. *Psychoanalytic Study of the Child 22*: 162–86.

Brim, O. G. (1965) Adolescent personality as self-other systems. *Journal of Marriage and the Family 27*: 156–62.

Bronfenbrenner, U. (1974) The roots of alienation. *Scientific American 231*: 53–61.

Bronson, G. A. (1959) Identity diffusion in late adolescence. *Journal of Abnormal and Social Psychology 59*: 414–17.

Coleman, J. C. (1974) *Relationships in Adolescence*. London: Routledge and Kegan Paul.

Coleman, J. C. (1978) Current contradictions in adolescent theory. *Journal of Youth and Adolescence 7*: 1–11.

Coleman, J. C. (1979) Friendship and the peer group. In J. Adelson (ed.) *Handbook of Adolescent Psychology*. New York: John Wiley.

Coleman, J. C., George, R. and Holt, G. (1977) Adolescents and their parents: a study of attitudes. *Journal of Genetic Psychology 130*: 239–45.

Coleman, J. C., Herzberg, J. and Morris, M. (1977) Identity in adolescence: present and future self-concepts. *Journal of Youth and Adolescence 6*: 63–75.

Douvan, E. and Adelson, J. (1966) *The Adolescent Experience*. New York: John Wiley.

Elder, G. H. (1968) Adolescent socialization and development. In E. Borgatta and W. Lambert (eds) *Handbook of Personality Theory and Research*. Chicago: Rand McNally.

Elder, G. H. (1975) Adolescence in the life cycle. In S. E. Dragastin and G. H. Elder (eds) *Adolescence in the Life Cycle*. New York: John Wiley.

Engel, M. (1959) The stability of the self-concept in adolescence. *Journal of Abnormal and Social psychology 58*: 211–15.

Erikson, E. H. (1963) *Childhood and Society*. New York: Norton.

Erikson, E. H. (1968) *Identity: Youth and Crisis*. London: Faber and Faber.

Freud, A. (1937) *The Ego and the Mechanisms of Defence*. London: Hogarth Press.

Gustafson, B. (1972) *Life Values of High School Youth in Sweden*. Stockholm: Institute of Sociology of Religion.

Howard, L. P. (1960) Identity conflicts in adolescent girls. *Smith College Studies in Social Work 31*: 1–24.

Jennings, M. and Niemi, R. (1975) Continuity and change in political orientations – a longitudinal study of two generations. *American Political Science Review 69*: 1316–35.

Mahler, M. S. (1963) Thoughts about development and individuation. *Psychoanalytic Study of the Child 18*: 307–24.

Monge, R. H. (1973) Developmental trends in factors of adolescent self-concept. *Developmental Psychology 8*: 382–93.

Nesselroade, J. and Baltes, P. (1974) Adolescent personality: development and historical change. *Monographs for the Society of Research in Child Development 39*: 154.

Offer, D. (1969) *The Psychological World of the Teenager*. New York: Basic Books.

Offer, D. and Offer, J. (1975) *From Teenage to Young Manhood*. New York: Basic Books.

Piers, E. V. and Harris, D. B. (1964) Age and other correlates of self-concept in children. *Journal of Educational Psychology 55*: 91–5.

Rosenberg, M. (1965) *Society and the Adolescent Self-Image*. Princeton, N. J.: Princeton University Press.

Rutter, M., Graham, P., Chadwick, O. and Yule, W. (1976) Adolescent turmoil: fact or fiction? *Journal of Child Psychology and Psychiatry 17*: 35–56.

Simmons, R., Rosenberg, F., and Rosenberg, M. (1973) Disturbance in the self-image at adolescence. *American Sociological Review 38*: 553–68.

Tomé, H. R. (1972) *Le moi et l'autre dans la conscience de l'adolescence*. Paris: Delachaux & Niestlé.

Westley, W. A. and Elkin, F. (1957) The protective environment and adolescent socialization. *Social Forces 35*: 243–9.

2 The development of self

Christopher Wilson

Introduction

The concept of self has had a long and contentious history within
psychology and philosophy alike. Controversies have centred on three
major questions: 'How does a person become aware of his or her
existence?', 'Does self-consciousness govern or reflect an individual's
behaviour?' and 'Can self-awareness be studied scientifically?'.

David Hume (1739) argued that there was no certain evidence of
self. Most of us, though, are sure of our own existence and this chapter
attempts to show how this knowledge of self arises and develops.

The second question, of whether consciousness governs or merely
registers our actions, is beyond the scope of such a short chapter.
However, we can briefly suggest that the evidence shows a reciprocal
flow of cause and effect. Consciousness influences behaviour and vice
versa. Regardless of its power in governing behaviour, self-consciousness has obvious importance in showing the imprint of socialization
and the way that society is impressed upon us and lives within us.

Since self is of extraordinary concern and importance to most
people, it seems strange that many psychologists have been reluctant
to study experience and self-awareness. From the 1920s onwards the
behaviourists have questioned the validity of studying self. They felt
that psychology should adopt the scrupulous methodology of the
physical sciences and rejected experience on the grounds that it was

not amenable to objective, scientific scrutiny. The behaviourists believed that psychology should gather objective data by examining behaviour rather than thought and experience. Two criticisms of the behaviourist arguments are obvious. Firstly, it is perverse and self-contradictory to offer a subjective critique of subjectivity. Secondly, the data obtained by asking people to talk about themselves is as behavioural as any other. Talking is as much a behaviour as the movement of furry mammal limbs in a Skinner-box: neither can be sampled objectively, for both are sensed and monitored in the experience of the experimenter. Rosenthal (1966) has shown us that behaviourist findings may be strongly influenced by the biases, experiences and expectations of the mythically objective experimenter.

As we shall see later in the chapter, there are striking similarities between the minds of behaviourists and young children; for both are primarily concerned with behaviour and objective reality and have difficulty understanding the nature of subjectivity, self and experience. Children become progressively aware of the nature of mind; it is to be hoped that professional psychologists may be able to make similar progress.

Those researchers concerned with self have generated a variety of overlapping concepts and definitions. The simplest, clearest and least presumptuous definition of self seems to be that of Murphy (1947): 'The self is the individual as known to the individual'. *Self* and *self-concept* are used interchangeably in the literature to refer to an individual's overall self-awareness. The concept of *identity* overlaps, but is employed to refer to a self that is conscious of the possibility for future development and receptive to the demands and expectations of other people (McCandless and Evans, 1973).

The self has three major components. The individual becomes aware of personal characteristics, but also judges them and assesses their power. *Self-esteem* and *self-valuation* refer to the individual's judgement of his worth. Such an estimate is not based on a single dimension but reflects a variety of transitory or stable feelings – pride, guilt, shame, acceptance, rejection, success, failure, popularity, status. *Sense of personal power* describes the individual's assessment of his power and effectiveness in influencing his world. Frequently, this sense is described in terms of *locus of control* (Rotter, 1966; Lefcourt, 1976; Phares, 1976). Those people with an *internal* locus of control see themselves as powerful agents acting and imposing on their world. In simple terms, they are existentialists who feel they are largely responsible for their own destiny. In contrast, those who feel that control is *external* to them are fatalists, feeling that they are tossed and turned by the ebb and flow of forces beyond their control.

Changes of self appear to be qualitative rather than gradual and cumulative. So, to understand the self that the child first brings to school, we must examine development from birth. This account attempts to describe four stages in the revolutionary changes in self. The child first discovers his body, then his mind, then the differences between his own and other people's minds. In a fourth stage, at adolescence, the individual is faced with the task of developing a coherent, independent, productive and sexual self to deploy in the uncertain future of adult life. The nature of self in the four stages is summarized below.

Stage 1. Discovery of the bodily self

(a) *Self-awareness.* The infant discovers his own body and distinguishes it from the bodies of other people and other objects, learns the permanence of his own body and creates a personal symbol of self. With the acquisition of language, the child learns to describe and elaborate this symbol of the bodily self.

(b) *Self-evaluation.* The child values the bodily self in terms of the pleasure and pain associated with it.

(c) *Sense of personal power.* The child becomes aware that his own body, other people's bodies and objects have power in making things happen.

Stage 2. Discovery of the psychological self

(a) *Self-awareness.* Gradually the child learns to distinguish impulses, thoughts, perceptions and feelings from the people and objects that provoke them. The child recognizes his mind and learns that his experiences differ from those of other people.

(b) *Self-evaluation.* The acquisition of guilt, shame and pride, and awareness of other people's like and dislike, provide the child with new dimensions on which to judge his worth.

(c) *Sense of personal power.* The child learns to distinguish the powers of animate and inanimate matter and learns that names and thoughts do not have the same potency as their referents. Awareness of personal power changes as the child grows more adept but recognizes the competing abilities of parents and peers.

Stage 3. Discovery of the schizoid self

(a) *Self-awareness*. Having learned of the psychological differences between self and others, the child recognizes the variety of ways of being a person and responds to the varying demands of parents, peers and teachers. The child develops a schizoid, multi-faceted self with domestic, achieving and sociable components.

(b) *Self-evaluation*. The child increasingly judges self in terms of the reactions of peers, on the basis of popularity, achievement and status.

(c) *Sense of personal power*. The child's estimate of personal effectiveness will vary with success in competing and cooperating with peers.

Stage 4. The adolescent self

(a) *Self-awareness*. The adolescent acquires the ability for propositional, intellectual thought, develops a mature sexual body and tackles social and personal demands for increased independence.

(b) *Self-evaluation*. The adolescent extends judgements of his value in terms of other people's reactions to his or her sexual characteristics, and in relation to confidence and success in achieving adult identity.

(c) *Sense of personal power*. The adolescent's sense of effectiveness grows with increasing physical and intellectual parity with adults. Sense of power also increases as the adolescent is offered a large measure of self-determination in planning a future.

Chapter 4 shows that sexual identity is too potent and pervasive to ignore. Even pronouns have sex, so it is difficult to describe self-awareness without implying gender. Though this chapter attempts to show the development of self in girls and boys alike, I have followed convention in describing the ambiguous – male or female – third person as a 'he'. Paradoxically, it is difficult to avoid sex without appearing sexist.

The bodily self

The newborn infant seems aware of the world but ignorant of self. Sensitivity to touch, sight, sound, smell and changes of body position is evident at birth. Shortly after, the sense of taste develops, flavouring the world.

Though the infant seems genetically pre-programmed to attend to certain visual features – faces, depth, etc. – he does not show any evidence of memory until about 10 weeks old (Brackbill, 1971). Until then, when the infant is able to detect regularities and consistencies of sensation, the world will be a constant flux of novel ingredients.

Gradually, through memory, the child recognizes consistency in the world and discriminates between people and objects, recognizing clusters of sensations as whole and separate things. As the infant learns that the world is composed of discrete things, he will also learn that his own body is amongst these. There are several reasons why the infant will inevitably encounter his body and distinguish it from the rest of the world. When an object meets the infant's body it will evoke sense of touch; when it strikes something else, there will be no awareness of touch. Further evidence of the existence and boundaries of the body will be provided by the child's own actions. Acting on his own body, the child will obtain a duplicity of tactile stimulation – from the mouth that sucks and from the finger that is sucked, for example. In contrast, he will obtain only singular touches when acting on other objects. The saliency of the child's own body (the fact that actions on it evoke strong feelings of pleasure and pain) will also focus attention on the somatic self. As the child gains mobility he will learn that his body, this rich source of touch, pleasure and pain, is the most regular feature of his world; for wherever the child goes, he takes his body with him.

Gradually, the child seems to recognize the comparability of his own body to the bodies of other people and imitates their actions – initially only modelling with those portions of his body (hands, arms, legs) that are visible to him. With the development of imitative and other visually guided movements the child watches the actions of his own body and begins to recognize its power to make things happen.

Until about 9 months of age, the child does not seem to impute permanence to objects in his world. His knowledge of the existence of things is dependent on his immediate perception of them (Mussen et al., 1974). Apparently, if the child does not sense something then he does not conceive of its existence. Though recognizing the repetition of past events, the child does not infer their continuity, i.e. is unaware that he or the world have any future. Just as the child is aware of objects only when he meets them, he is, presumably, only conscious of the bodily self on the frequent occasions when he encounters it.

Although the young child is unaware of the permanence of his body, the feelings evoked by it have a lasting impact on self-valuation. The quality of the parent's initial care of the child has been shown to influence self-esteem over eleven years later. For example, Coopersmith (1967) found that boys who were bottle fed had slightly greater self-esteem at age 12 than those who were breast fed. The boys who had suffered infantile frustration in being changed from breast to bottle feeding had the lowest self-esteem.

The child's ability, developing after the age of about 9 months, to ascribe continuity to objects beyond their sensory persistence is derived from symbolic representations of the world (Piaget, 1951). Piaget has shown that the child is able, by developing and elaborating these symbols, to search for hidden objects, predict the path of objects beyond sight, imitate absent models. Just as the child acquires symbols for other people, objects and events, so he develops symbolic representation of his bodily self. Having already been created by his parents, the child can create himself – making himself in his own image through a personal symbol of self. By the age of 12 months, the symbol enables the child to recognize himself from his mirror image, and he will studiously manipulate the image by moving various parts of his body (Dixon, 1957). This response is different from that of younger children – who ignore their image or smile at it as if it were a playmate. Having acquired personal symbols, the child is capable of learning the community's symbols – words.

Perhaps the earliest and most basic influence of the child's language on his self-conception will be in reinforcing the lessons of infancy: that he is separate from other people and objects with whom he shares common space. The child's own words, or mere babbles, will allow him to hear himself act, see others respond to him, and will reinforce his sense of personal existence and effectiveness.

Typically, the child first refers to self as he is referred to by others – by Christian name – before learning the use of 'I' or 'me' (Ames, 1952). Even having learned his name, the child's sense of self may be intermittent. The child that can name others may have difficulty or hesitancy in pointing to self by name (Agnew and Bannister, 1976). The child does not appear to be continually self-aware, but recognizes himself from sensations of his own body and from other people's references to him.

William James (1890) suggested that a large component of the individual's sense of self is defined by personal possessions. By the age of about 2 years the child has become a colonist, extending sense of self beyond the body and staking claims on the world with the possessive pronoun 'mine' (Ames, 1952). The communal awareness implicit in the use of 'us' and 'ours' is not usually expressed until about 3 years of age. By this time, the child has reinforced his sense of correspondence to others and has gained the generalist self-descriptions of sex, age and skin colour (Ausubel and Sullivan, 1970).

The child's speech reveals him to be 'egocentric' in several respects. Self-centredness is reflected in the child's tendency to talk primarily to himself about himself. From the ages of about 18 months to 2 years, the child's speech consists largely of monologues addressed to the self which serve to describe, confirm and elaborate his sense of existence. The monologues do not restrict the child's social experience, though, for he is also egocentric in assuming that everyone and everything share his thoughts, feelings and perceptions (Piaget, 1929). Until the child learns that nobody shares his head, talking to the self will be remarkably like talking to other people.

Language will ultimately undermine childish egocentrism in two ways. Firstly, the child will learn through discussion and disagreement that other people do not share his own perceptions, thoughts and feelings. Secondly, the symbols of language can be applied upon themselves, in thinking about thought, to explain and reconcile the disagreements of conversation. Paradoxically, although language will inevitably counter self-centredness, early language learning reinforces and encourages the child's egocentric view. Consider the problem of teaching language to the child, which revolves around naming the unknown. The child has experiences, you have words: you want to teach him that the words in your head are applicable to the experiences within his. To teach him to label objects, you must support his egocentrism by adopting or anticipating his perceptual stance – saying 'cat' when you think he is looking at a cat. The child learns two lessons simultaneously: that cat refers to a particular type of object and that other people see cat when he does. In teaching the child to label his emotions, you must act as a behaviourist and define them in terms of his behaviour and context. When the child cries after several hours without food, you call him 'hungry'. He is encouraged, then, to view hunger as a feature of the world rather than as an experience within the privacy of his own body.

The acquisition of language inevitably encourages childish egocentrism, for words can only be taught by anticipating and reinforcing the child's perceptual and emotional stance. As long as the child assumes that perceptions and experiences are shared, he will be unable to distinguish the objective and the subjective and will continue to define self in physical rather than psychological terms.

The psychological self

Infants live in a privileged and permissive society. Tulkin and Kagan (1972) have shown that over 90 per cent of maternal behaviour towards 10-month-old infants consists of affection, play and care-taking. Attempts to control or prohibit the infant's behaviour accounted for only 5 per cent of the mother's acts. However, as the child becomes more competent and mobile, his impulsiveness becomes an inconvenience to parents and a danger to self. Accordingly, by the age of 18 months to 2 years, the child is subjected to a remarkable turn-about in maternal behaviour. Mother, who had previously developed her child's attachment through intensive attention, care and play, begins to use this attachment to control and restrict the child's move-ment. Minton et al. (1971) have shown that 65 per cent of the inter-actions between mothers and their 2-year-old children involve attempts by the mother to control the child's behaviour against his will, and in 60 per cent of these instances the child complied or was forced to comply. Hoffman (1977) observed even more intense discipline in the relationship of mothers and their $3\frac{1}{2}$-year-old kids, calculating that the children experienced maternal pressure to change their behaviour every six to eight minutes of their waking life. Parents are difficult to satisfy and demand progressively greater control and achievement of the child.

In loosing their barrage of discipline, parents try to teach the child to recognize that his impulses – source and impetus of his actions – lie within him, are a source of personal power and a determinant of his value. Impulse, then, is likely to become the first component of the child's psychic self – the first aspect of psychological individuality to be recognized.

The parents' effectiveness in teaching the child to recognize and control his own impulses will depend on the type of discipline that they employ. Hoffman (1970, 1977) has characterized parental discipline as being of three basic forms: 'power assertion', 'love withdrawal' and 'induction'. Power assertion refers to physical punishment, threats and deprivation of material rewards. In withdrawing love, the parent states dislike of the child or ignores him. In employing induction, the parent gives reasons or explanations for the child to change his behaviour, and points out the consequences of acts for self and others.

In reviewing a large body of evidence, Hoffman concludes that the mother's use of induction leads the child to internalize the parent's values and to experience guilt when tempted to violate this morality. Mother's power assertion teaches the child to fear detection and punishment – to conceal aspects of self. Withdrawal of love leads the child to inhibit anger, but otherwise does not seem consistently related to moral behaviour.

If the child's impulses become a consistent source of anxiety to him he may become intolerant of them and deny their access to consciousness (Mussen et al., 1974). Though parental discipline is usually intended to teach the child to recognize his own impulses, it may teach him to deny or evade these problematic aspects of self. Hoffman (1977) suggests that parents who tend to use a combination of love withdrawal and induction are particularly likely to make their children intolerant of their own impulses.

Besides influencing self-awareness, discipline will affect the child's self-valuation and sense of personal power. Power assertion carries a latent message from parent to child – 'Your wishes are unimportant' – and is a recipe for low self-esteem. Love withdrawal will induce insecurity and conditional self-worth by expressing the message 'I only love you when you are good'. Love withdrawal and power assertion also encourage low self-valuation by teaching the child the self-descriptive labels of 'bad' and 'naughty' – labels which acquire punishing properties in their own right through association with physical punishment or rejection. Induction, in contrast to the other two techniques, encourages high self-valuation in stressing to the child that his behaviours and impulses are important to parents, self and others. Not surprisingly, then, Coopersmith (1967) found that boys subjected to a parental discipline of love withdrawal or physical punishment had lower self-esteem when tested at the age of 12 than boys who had received more inductive control. Coopersmith also observed that consistent, effective parental discipline led the boys to hold high self-valuations. Presumably these children were spared the recurrent pain and negative evaluations that stem from frequent and unpredictable punishment.

One consequence of parental discipline will be the child's conception of an 'ideal-self' that can reconcile and meet the conflicting demands of self and parents. Since induction leads the child to internalize parental values, it will also lead to a strong correspondence of the self and ideal-self. Withdrawal of love and power assertion both teach the child that he is relatively impotent in comparison to his parents, and encourages a sense of fatalism, of being more acted upon than

acting. The child that has been brought-up under a regime of induction, conversely, will be prompted to feel the primary agent in his own
actions; for the parents emphasize the importance and consequences of
the child's own actions and make appeals to his pride and self-control.
In trying to explain the effectiveness of induction, Hoffman (1977)
refers to the distinction between episodic and semantic memory.
Episodic memory refers to the retention of the source and context of a
message as a single personally experienced event: semantic memory
refers to a permanent system of linguistically based knowledge.
Induction helps the child to incorporate moral standards into his
semantic memory. He may attribute them to himself – internalize
them – having forgotten the particular occasion upon which they were
imposed by his parents.

We can summarize the egocentric child's self-awareness as being
'inside-out'. Since all knowledge is subjective, sensory in origin, it is
difficult to gain a concept of objectivity. Until the child is able to
distinguish experiences and the 'things' that cause them he will continue to regard his experience as public and lying beyond his body.
Experience is inevitably located outside the bodily self, since everything that is seen and touched appears to lie on or beyond the frontier
of the child's skin.

The child is perceptually and cognitively egocentric, unaware that
his view of the world is inside and private, rather than outside and
public. As a consequence of this egocentrism the child exhibits an all
encompassing empathy, assuming that others share his perception,
feelings and thoughts. The child believes – or has never thought to
doubt – that there is a moral uniformity in the world, assuming that
everyone shares the moral standards that he personally acquired from
his parents. The empathy extends even to objects; the child 'animist-
ally' believes that they too have experiences like his and will intervene
to punish him if he contravenes the absolute morality of the world
(Piaget, 1929).

Since the child assumes that others share his perceptions and
thoughts, he is unaware of their alternative views and different
knowledge. He is egocentric in taking the role of another person,
supposing that others must share his view of a situation. Until he can
discriminate between an object and his symbols, perceptions and
thoughts of it, experiences and their referents will be inextricably confused and compounded. As William James (1890) suggested, the child
must learn that whilst dogs may bite the name 'dog' does not.

Dreams and fantasy are also confused with public reality. If the child cannot recognize the individuality of his own experience, he will regard dreams as events within a shared world. There is a Chinese legend of a man who falls asleep and, on waking, cannot decide if he is a man who dreamed he was a butterfly or a butterfly who now dreams he is a man. The egocentric child has similar difficulties in reconciling the contradictory worlds of sleep and wakefulness, particularly since he treats the two as equally real.

Piaget (1929) has shown that the child's confusion of the private and public leads to unrealistic conceptions of personal power. By the age of 2 years the child has learned that he personally, and other people, can make things happen, and that objects and people influence each other through contact in time and space. However, even at the age of 7, the egocentric child has not learned to distinguish between the powers of animate and lifeless matter. The child projects his impulses and feelings onto objects – believing that they share a power that is, in fact, his own.

Since he cannot distinguish between symbols and their referents, the child confuses objects and their effects with the names and thoughts by which he refers to them. Consequently, the symbols are assumed to share of the power of their referents; the child believes that by changing his words and thoughts he can transform the object itself.

In short, the child's 'egocentric magic' (Piaget, 1929) shows a simultaneous overestimate and underestimate of personal power. The child underestimates his power by believing that he is subject to the will and impulses of inanimate matter, and flatters himself by trying, like Uri Geller or King Canute, to change matter by thought alone.

The concept of objectivity – the awareness of a 'real' world that is inconsistently sampled by perception – involves distinguishing thoughts, perceptions and symbols from the 'things' to which they refer. The concept is acquired by turning subjectivity upon itself – by experiencing experience and thinking about thought.

There are two prerequisites for this attainment of objectivity. The child must have the fodder and capacity for self-conscious thought. The food for this thought is provided by inconsistencies within the child's view of the world and by contradictions between his own and other people's descriptions of things. The capacity for self-conscious thought – the ability to apply thought to itself – seems to be acquired at the age of about 6 or 7 years, when the child progresses from 'pre-operational' to 'concrete operational' thought (Piaget, 1950). The

perception and thought of the preoperational child tends to be 'centred', biased by a single, striking feature of the stimulus to the exclusion of balancing and counteracting aspects. So, for example, a preoperational child may be unable to recognize his sister because she is wearing new clothes. Subsequently, in the stage of concrete operational thought, the child is capable of making more balanced judgements, able to think about his judgements and reverse the logic by which he reached them. By thinking about his thought, the concrete operational child will be able to recognize and reconcile disagreements between himself and others, realize that he has idiosyncratic perceptions of a 'real' world and so learn to locate perceptions and thoughts within himself rather than within a common world beyond. Rubin (1973) and Cowan (1966) have shown that the various forms of the child's egocentrism – perceptual, communicative and role-taking – are strongly interrelated and positively associated with the centration of perception. Objectivity is attained with concrete operational thought. The self becomes conscious of its consciousness; the ego is well on its trip.

Selman (1971) identified four stages in the process by which the child learns objectivity, recognizes the idiosyncracy of his own perceptions and takes the role of another person. In a stage of initial awareness, the child recognizes the individuality of his perceptions but still confuses them with those of other people. In a second stage, the child seems to over-apply the lesson of his own individuality and fails to see any correspondence between his own and the other person's experience. Then, the child is able to attribute his own view to others by hypothetically putting himself in their position. Finally, the child becomes aware that the other person has views or reasoning that may, or may not, be similar to his own. Selman's findings show that the recognition of perceptual and cognitive individuality develops considerably between the ages of 4 and 7, and continues to grow thereafter. As Chandler and Greenspan (1972) and Kurdek and Rodgon (1975) have shown, the child's egocentricity and inaccuracy in anticipating the view of another person continues to decrease between the age of 6 and 13 years.

Even when the child has become self-conscious of his thoughts and perceptions, and has incorporated them within his model of self, he continues to define self in material terms (Piaget, 1929). It takes the child a long time to learn that there are aspects of the world and of the self that are not solid or touchable. At the age of about 6, the

child typically conceives of his thought as being a solid thing, sub-
stantiated in language and situated in the mouth that voices it or ear
that hears it. By the age of 7 or 8, the child learns that thought lies
between his ears – within the head – but continues to regard it as a
material thing. Not until 11 or 12 years of age does the child cease to
think of thoughts as being a substance. Just as the child learns the
insubstantiality of thought, so he comes to realize that dreams are not
real, material events either (Piaget, 1929).

The schizoid self

As the child's objectivity increases he discovers new, psychological
criteria of his individuality by locating feelings, thoughts and perceptions within self. On losing the promiscuous empathy of egocentrism,
the child is simultaneously able to recognize and respond to the
individuality of others. Understandably, then, the self becomes increasingly 'individuated' between the ages of 6 and 12 – the child
grows to view himself as increasingly different to other people (Long
et al., 1968).

From his first arrival at school, the child has led a 'schizoid', split,
compartmentalized life – responding in turns to the varying demands
or expectations of parents, peers and teachers. In losing his egocentrism, between the ages of 7 and 13, the child is progressively able
to recognize the distinctive features of these three types of people, and
will develop various models of self from their varying demands. In
Cooley's terms (1918), the child will develop 'looking glass selves' in
the reflections of the differing responses and expectations of those
about him. The child is likely to develop and distinguish three distinct
types of self: a domestic self for parents, an achieving self for teachers
and a sociable self for peers.

We have already discussed those aspects of the child's self that
parents will accentuate and emphasize. The child will learn from his
parents that he is a valued but relatively weak dependant who is
expected to show self-control in regulating his own behaviour.

Parents exert a strong influence on their children's self-valuations.
Children with high self-esteem tend to have parents who are warm
(Sears, 1970), who value themselves and their offspring highly, who
feel that the child should be democratically involved in home
decisions, and who regard their children as a natural outcome of
marriage (Coopersmith, 1967). It is an occupational hazard of being a

child to discover that your parents wanted offspring that were better or different. Demanding parents, feeling that they have lost in the lottery of reproduction, may implicitly tell their children that they are of the wrong sex or defective quality.

The same-sex parent offers the child an appropriate model of how to be and be effective, and between the ages of 6 and 12 the child shows a slight increase in identification with the parental model (Long et al., 1968). Identification with friends, though, increases to a far greater extent over this period. In losing egocentrism, and in mixing increasingly with other people from a variety of backgrounds, the child becomes progressively aware of the many ways of being a person. Correspondingly, the extent to which children value themselves for being like their parents changes with age. Between 6 and 8 years of age, children would ideally like to be like members of their families. Subsequently the child increasingly describes his ideal self as being like a glamorous person outside the family or as being an amalgam of the best features of several different people (Havighurst et al., 1946). The girl who initially wanted to be like mum may, on more mature reflection, decide that there would be a greater premium on combining the ability of Chris Evert, the allure of Mata Hari, the mind of Albert Einstein and the jewellery of Liberace.

Parents and teachers both encourage the child to define self in terms of achievement by stressing the importance of success in class. Mothers encourage performance by spontaneously rewarding the child's achievements, by resisting childish demands for excessive help and by allowing the child an active involvement in family activities and decisions (Crandall, 1963; Mussen et al., 1974). Teachers similarly encourage an achieving self by showing personal warmth, encouragement and a democratic approach to the child's participation in class (Mussen et al., 1974).

Leviton (1975) has reviewed a large body of research examining the relationship of school performance and self-valuation. The evidence consistently shows a moderate, positive correlation. Brookover et al. (1967), for example, found that the correlation of self-esteem and academic achievement ranged between $+ \cdot 46$ and $+ \cdot 63$ for a range of high school children, falling below $+ \cdot 50$ only when they neared the end of their schooling. Obviously if parents place a strong emphasis on school achievement the child may well use this criterion in recognizing or calculating his own value. At school the child is usually subjected to the glare of ordinal distinctions, and will be able to continually chart his progress in relation to that of his peers. Accordingly, children tend to be particularly accurate in judging their abilities. Coopersmith (1967) has shown that whilst mothers tend to over-estimate their child's ability, he knows better and evaluates himself more realistically.

The relationship of achievement and self-esteem reflects reciprocal cause and effect. Achievement boosts self-esteem; initially low self-esteem inhibits achievement. In the remorseless cycle of the self-fulfilling prophecy, success and failure sustain themselves. Those who bring a low self-esteem to school tend to be anxious about their performance and their general worth (Hamachek, 1965) and this anxiety interferes with academic achievement (Sharma, 1970).

Clearly, as the child grows up, gains skills and knowledge and moves from the authoritarian control of parents to the relatively democratic society of peers, he will see his personal power as being in the ascendant. Understandably Beebe (1971) found that children feel an increasing sense of personal power between the ages of 6 and 16 years. Milgram (1971) has confirmed this growing sense of effectiveness in children aged between 10 and 16. The sense of autonomy and control is associated with high self-esteem. The child who perceives himself as being more controlling than controlled is likely to value himself highly (Epstein and Komorita, 1971).

Popularity amongst school children is influenced by their enthusiasm, out-going nature, cheerfulness, friendliness (Bonney, 1943, 1944; Mussen et al., 1974). The evidence confirms the commonsense view that children seek each other for friendliness and play. Peer groups develop their own norms which are, to some extent, incidental to, and independent of, those of parents and teachers (Hartup, 1970; Stone and Church, 1968) and enforce these norms by ridiculing deviants. Understandably, then, older children show a measure of conformity to group norms (Berenda, 1950) – a conformity that is absent or barely evident in younger, egocentric children (Hunt and Synnerdale, 1959; Stone and Church, 1968).

Self-acceptance consistently relates to acceptance by others (Wylie, 1961). Popular children tend to have higher self-esteem than their unpopular peers (Coopersmith, 1967; Ziller et al., 1964). With popularity as with academic achievement, nothing succeeds like failure. The experience and expectation of rejection confirms itself. Rejection lowers self-esteem (Ziller, 1973) and low self-esteem inhibits the formation of friendships (Bonney, 1943, 1944; Mussen et al., 1974).

Piaget has shown that the child's moral values and self-valuations undergo a qualitative change after the age of about 7, as a consequence of diminished egocentrism and increased interaction with peers (Piaget, 1932; Hoffman, 1977). As the child grows aware of the diversity of possible views of the world, he ceases to believe that the moral values expressed by his parents are immutably and absolutely binding. Instead the child adopts a morality based on reciprocity, cooperation and consensus with peers. The child sees rules as being sustained by general agreement, but flexibly adaptable to individual needs. Judgements of goodness and badness are increasingly based on the intentions behind acts, rather than on consequences. The child believes that punishment should serve the restitution of harm. Having progressively moved from the company of parents, the child grows aware that punishment is not an inevitable, painful consequence of wrong-doing. Having lost his egocentric, animistic empathy with the lifeless, the child realizes that objects do not collude in imposing a relentless morality on the world.

Now, the child's moral imperatives are to conform to the expectations and norms of peers, and to show consideration for others by placing himself in their position. The child values himself, and is valued by his peers, by the extent to which he observes these standards.

The adolescent self

The sense of self in adolescence seems regressive in some respects. The individual shows a renewed tendency to define the self in bodily terms and exhibits a resurgence of egocentrism. These changes can be traced to three major causes: physical development, demands for adult identity and intellectual development.

From the age of about 11 onwards, the child shows a qualitative advance in intellectual functioning which places him on a par with parents, teachers and other adults. The child becomes capable of 'formal operations' (Piaget, 1950). Thought is freed from the practicalities of concrete events and is capable of formulating and conceiving the possible as well as the real. Hypothetico-deductive and propositional thought are developed and the adolescent, though inferior in experience, has the potential to deal with adults on terms of intellectual equality.

Early adolescence is marked literally and metaphorically by a resurgence of the body. The adolescent watches his or her body spurt into growth and develop secondary sexual characteristics. As a result of these changes, the self is increasingly interested in and defined by the body. Whereas the infant values his body in terms of its pleasure and pain, the adolescent's body derives value in social and symbolic terms from the reactions of others.

The community places value on the physical development of the adolescent, who judges self in the reflection of these responses – feeling rejected or of low value if the body does not conform to the social ideal (Jones, 1938; Mussen et al., 1974). Late-maturing boys score significantly lower in their self-valuations than their early developing peers (Weatherly, 1964). For adolescent girls the relationship of sexual development and self-esteem is less clear. Popularity and self-valuation are less clearly and consistently tied to the speed of the body in developing mature sexual features (Lynn, 1959; Faust, 1960).

The sexual body of the adolescent wields power on several dimensions. For the self inside it, the body provokes novel feelings and motives. For others that watch it, the body attracts. Socially, the sexual maturity is a metaphor for the adolescent's growing parity with adults. The body is also proscribed; for the society that admires it simultaneously tells its owner that sexual mores restrict its direct and natural use. One problem for adolescents, then, is that the community simultaneously emphasizes and frustrates the power of their bodies.

The adolescent can respond to sexual guilt and anxiety by repressing the body (Group for the Advancement of Psychiatry, 1968), can sublimate its power, or find outlet through masturbation and intercourse. Historically, in the UK and US at least, the sexual predicament of the adolescent is lessening. Though masturbation has been sustained at a fairly constant rate, associated guilt and anxiety have decreased. Premarital intercourse amongst adolescents has increased in recent decades, and the middle classes have been particularly enterprising in this regard (Mussen et al., 1974).

As the adolescent grows, physically and intellectually, to resemble the adult, personal and social demands for independence increase. Conflicts arise from both forms of demand. Though parents and teachers expect increasing maturity and autonomy from adolescents, they try to dictate the speed at which these are achieved – resisting extreme or early bids for independence. For the adolescent, as for others, autonomy is double-faced: attractive and threatening. As Fromm (1941) and Blos (1962) indicate, the prospective rewards of freedom are clouded by the uncertainty of achieving them and by the threat of losing the security of the known.

The adolescent is all dressed-up – in adult clothes, body and intellect – with too many places to go. There are simultaneously sexual, intellectual and independent aspects of self to be discovered, explored and defined. On these three dimensions the adolescent has the potential, but not the experience, to form a cohesive and balanced self. Accordingly, Erikson (1968) has described adolescence as a time of 'identity crisis' in which the individual must shape a positive, industrious, sociable and forward-looking self from the flux of personal change. The adolescent is faced with a plastic future in which the options seem almost unlimited and the outcomes unclear.

On the basis of Erikson's theory and his own research, Marcia (1966; 1970) has described four states of adolescent identity, suggesting that identity may be 'achieved', 'fore-closed', 'diffused' or 'in moratorium'. Achieved identity refers to a self that has experienced a crisis but has emerged triumphant with stable commitments, goals and ideology. An individual with a 'fore-closed' identity has avoided the uncertainties and anxieties of crisis and flux by rapidly committing himself to safe, conservative, conventional goals without exploring the many options open to self. The adolescent with a diffused identity is in crisis, unable to formulate a clear self-definition, goals or commitments. Erikson proposed that the society allows, and the adolescent accepts, a 'psychosocial moratorium' – a time in which identity decisions are held in abeyance whilst the individual can, without committing himself, try out and think out potential forms of self, lingering at the crossroad deciding on the path to take from childhood to adulthood. As we shall see, there is ample evidence that adolescents accept and utilize a moratorium but not that they typically experience a crisis of identity.

The adolescent's intellectual development, specifically his capacity for hypothetical thought, equip him for introspection and allow him to think out various existential options. Elkind (1967) has confirmed this tendency to introspection, and has shown that the adolescent's self-concern leads him to regress into egocentrism, to feel that others are thinking about him and feeling as he does himself. Besides hypothesizing about the future, the adolescent can experiment with various potential identities by manipulating his 'presentation of self' (Goffman, 1959). By contriving the information that he gives verbally, and gives off through gesture, appearance and manner, the individual can test the value and effectiveness of potential ways of being. Unfortunately, suggests Elkind, the adolescent performs to an imaginary audience; as a consequence of the prevailing egocentrism, everyone is an actor and none an audience in the theatre of adolescent showmanship.

The adolescent can also cope with anxiety about the future, holding decisions in abeyance, by losing himself in a variety of ways to different degrees. Anxiety about sexual aspects of self can be resisted by denying them access to consciousness or by intellectualizing them away. The adolescent's capacity for 'formal operations' equip him particularly well for more subtle forms of self-evasion. Transitory loss of self can be achieved by moving into diffuse gangs or crowds of peers in which there is a high degree of anonymity and a wide latitude of permissible behaviour (Yablonsky, 1967). Alcohol and other drugs enable the adolescent to use emblems of adult power, and allow evasion of self by reducing or altering consciousness. Affiliation to groups, gangs, youth movements and football clubs also provide self-avoidance. The adolescent can evade restrictions and low self-valuation by sharing more prestigious and powerful identities.

The possibilities for a 'moratorium' in the widest sense of the term, enabling the adolescent to experiment with identities and suspend, evade or delay problems of self-definition, can stave off crisis. Certainly, the evidence (e.g. Monge, 1973; Engel, 1959; Piers and Harris, 1964; Simmons et al., 1973) suggests that adolescents do not typically experience a crisis in defining or evaluating self. Findings by Coleman (1974) indicate that the adolescent is not overwhelmed in attempting to resolve simultaneously all areas of personal uncertainty, but, rather, focuses on problematic aspects of self in turn. Douvan and Adelson (1966) propose that the individual can defer problems of self by projecting them into the future. The adolescent, they argue, proposes a future-self to meet and resolve the requirements for personal change. Coleman et al. (1977) have validated and extended the idea, showing that during adolescence boys express increasing anxiety about their future self whilst manifesting a fairly constant anxiety about the existing self.

We have already seen the self develop beyond the school years. The problem of achieving a mature identity is shared by young adults (Toder and Marcia, 1973; Waterman, 1974). The difficulties confronting the adolescent in defining and adapting the sexuality, independence, power and value of self are experienced throughout life (Brim, 1966). The problem is called life, and demands constant revision of the individual's self-concept.

References

Agnew, J. and Bannister, D. (1976) The child's construing of self. *Nebraska Symposium on Motivation*: 99–127.

Ames, L. B. (1952) The sense of self of nursery children as manifested by their verbal behaviour. *Journal of Genetic Psychology 81*: 193–232.

Ausubel, D. P. and Sullivan, E. V. (1970) *Theory and Problems of Child Development* (second edition). New York: Grune and Stratton.

Beebe, J. S. (1971) Self-concept and internal–external control in children and adolescents. *Dissertation Abstracts International 31*: 4966A–67A.

Berenda, R. W. (1950) *The Influence of the Group on the Judgements of Children*. New York: King's Crown Press.

Blos, P. (1962) *On Adolescence*. London: Collier-Macmillan.

Bonney, M. E. (1943) The constancy of sociometric scores and their relationship to teacher judgements of social success and to personality self-ratings. *Sociometry 6*: 409–23.

Bonney, M. E. (1944) Sex differences in social success and personality traits. *Child Development 15*: 63–79.

Brackbill, Y. (1971) The role of the cortex in orienting: orienting reflex in an anencephalic infant. *Developmental Psychology 5*: 195–201.

Brim, O. G. (1966) Socialization through the life-cycle. In O. G. Brim and S. Wheeler *Socialization after Childhood: Two Essays*. New York: Wiley.

Brookover, W. B., Erikson, E. L. and Joiner, L. M. (1967) *Self-Concept of Ability and School Achievement, III*. East Lansing: US Office of Education.

Chandler, M. J. and Greenspan, S. (1972) Ersatz egocentrism: a reply to H. Borke. *Developmental Psychology 7*: 104–6.

Coleman, J. C. (1974) *Relationships in Adolescence*. London: Routledge and Kegan Paul.

Coleman, J. C., Herzberg, J. and Morris, M. (1977) Identity in adolescence: Present and future self-concepts. *Journal of Youth and Adolescence 6*: 63–75.

Cooley, C. H. (1918) *Social Process*. New York: Scribner's Press.

Coopersmith, S. (1967) *The Antecedents of Self-Esteem*. San Francisco: Freeman.

Cowan, P. A. (1966) Cognitive egocentrism and social interaction in children. *American Psychologist 21*: 623.

Crandall, V. J. (1963) Achievement. In H. W. Stevenson (ed.) *Child Psychology*. Chicago: University of Chicago Press.

Dixon, J. C. (1957) Development of self-recognition. *Journal of Genetic Psychology 9*: 251–6.

Douvan, E. and Adelson, J. (1966) *The Adolescent Experience*. New York: Wiley.

Elkind, D. (1967) Egocentrism in adolescence. *Child Development 38*: 1025–34.

Engel, M. (1959) The stability of self-concept in adolescence. *Journal of Abnormal and Social Psychology 58*: 211–15.

Epstein, R. and Komorita, S. S. (1971) Self-esteem, success-failure and locus of control in Negro children. *Developmental Psychology 4*: 2–8.

Erikson, E. H. (1968) *Identity: Youth and Crisis*. New York: Norton (London: Faber and Faber).

Faust, M. S. (1960) Developmental maturity as a determinant of prestige of adolescent girls. *Child Development 31*: 173–84.

44 The School Years

Fromm, E. (1941) *Escape from Freedom*. New York: Holt, Rinehart and Winston.

Goffman, E. (1959) *The Presentation of Self in Everyday Life*. Republished Harmondsworth: Penguin (1969).

Group for the Advancement of Psychiatry (1968) *Normal Adolescence*. New York: Scribners.

Hamachek, D. E. (1965) *Encounters with Self*. New York: Holt, Rinehart and Winston.

Hartup, W. W. (1970) Peer interaction and social organization. In P. H. Mussen (ed.) *Carmichael's Manual of Child Psychology*, vol. 2 (third edition). New York: Wiley.

Havighurst, R. J., Robinson, M. Z. and Dorr, M. (1946) The development of the ideal self in childhood and adolescence. *Journal of Educational Research* 40: 241–57.

Hoffman, M. L. (1970) Moral development. In P. H. Mussen (ed.) *Carmichael's Manual of Child Psychology*, vol. 2 (third edition). New York: Wiley.

Hoffman, M. L. (1977) Moral internalization: current theory and research. In L. Berkowitz (ed.) *Advances in Experimental Social Psychology* 10: 86–135.

Hume, D. (1739) *A Treatise of Human Nature*. Republished Harmondsworth: Penguin (1969).

Hunt, R. G. and Synnerdale, V. (1959) Social influences among kindergarten children. *Sociology and Social Research* 43: 171–4.

James, W. (1890) *Principles of Psychology*. New York: Holt.

Jones, H. E. (1938) The California adolescent growth study. *Journal of Educational Research* 31: 561–7.

Kurdek, L. A. and Rodgon, M. M. (1975) Perceptual, cognitive and affective perspective taking in kindergarten through sixth-grade children. *Developmental Psychology* 11: 533–4.

Lefcourt, H. M. (1976) *Locus of Control: Current Trends in Theory and Research*. New Jersey: Lawrence Erlbaum Associates.

Leviton, H. (1975) The implications of the relationship between self-concept and academic achievement. *Child Study Journal* 5: 25–35.

Long, B. H., Ziller, R. C. and Henderson, E. H. (1968) Developmental changes in the self-concept during adolescence. *School Review* 76: 210–30.

Lynn, D. B. (1959) A note on sex differences in the development of masculine and feminine identification. *Psychological Review* 46: 126–35.

Marcia, J. E. (1966) Development and validation of ego identity status. *Journal of Personality and Social Psychology* 3: 551–8.

Marcia, J. E. and Friedman, M. L. (1970) Ego identity status in college women. *Journal of Personality* 38: 249–63.

McCandless, B. R. and Evans, E. D. (1973) *Children and Youth: Psycho-Social Development*. Hinsdale, Illinois: Dryden Press.

Milgram, N. A. (1971) Locus of control in Negro and white children at four age levels. *Psychological Reports* 29: 459–65.

Minton, C., Kagan, J. and Levine, J. (1971) Maternal control and obedience in the two-year-old. *Child Development* 45: 299–304.

Monge, R. H. (1973) Developmental trends in factors of adolescent self-concept. *Developmental Psychology 8*: 382–93.

Murphy, G. (1947) *Personality*. New York: Harper.

Mussen, P. H., Conger, J. J. and Kagan, J. (1974) *Child Development and Personality* (fourth edition). New York: Harper and Row.

Phares, E. J. (1976) *Locus of Control in Personality*. Morristown, New Jersey: General Learning Press.

Piaget, J. (1929) *The Child's Conception of the World*. New York: Harcourt Brace.

Piaget, J. (1932) *The Moral Judgement of the Child*. London: Kegan Paul.

Piaget, J. (1950) *The Psychology of Intelligence*. New York: Harcourt Brace.

Piaget, J. (1951) *Play, Dreams and Imitation in Childhood*. New York: Norton.

Piers, E. V. and Harris, D. B. (1974) Age and other correlates of self-concept in children. *Journal of Educational Psychiatry 55*: 91–5.

Rosenthal, R. (1966) *Experimenter Effects in Behavioural Research*. New York: Appleton-Century-Crofts.

Rotter, J. B. (1966) Generalized expectancies for internal versus external control of reinforcement. *Psychological Monographs 80* (Whole no. 609).

Rubin, K. H. (1973) Egocentrism in childhood: a unitary construct? *Child Development 44*: 102–10.

Sears, R. R. (1970) Relation of early socialization experiences to self-concepts and gender role in middle childhood. *Child Development 41*: 267–90.

Selman, R. L. (1971) Taking another's perspective: role-taking development in early childhood. *Child Development 42*: 1721–34.

Sharma, S. (1970) Manifest anxiety and school achievement of adolescents. *Journal of Consulting and Clinical Psychology 34*: 403–7.

Simmons, R., Rosenberg, F. and Rosenberg, M. (1973) Disturbance in the self-image at adolescence. *American Sociological Review 38*: 553–68.

Stone, L. J. and Church, J. (1968) *Childhood and Adolescence*. New York: Random House.

Toder, N. L. and Marcia, J. E. (1973) Ego identity status and response to conformity pressure in college women. *Journal of Personality and Social Psychology 26*: 287–94.

Tulkin, S. R. and Kagan, J. (1972) Mother-infant interaction in the first year of life. *Child Development 43*: 31–42.

Waterman, A. S. and Waterman, C. K. (1974) A longitudinal study of changes in ego identity status during the freshman to senior year in college. *Developmental Psychology 10*: 387–92.

Weatherly, D. (1964) Self-perceived rate of physical maturation and personality in late adolescence. *Child Development 35*: 1197–210.

Wylie, R. (1961) *The Self-Concept*. Lincoln: University of Nebraska Press.

Yablonsky, L. (1967) *The Violent Gang*. Harmondsworth: Penguin.

Ziller, R. C. (1973) *The Social Self*. New York: Pergamon.

Ziller, R. C., Alexander, M. and Long, B. H. (1964) Self-social constructs and social desirability. Unpublished manuscript, University of Delaware.

3 Moral development

Helen Weinreich-Haste

Introduction

Moral development poses a number of problems for psychologists. Firstly, the definitions and categories of 'moral' are a mixture of folk wisdom and the heritage of philosophy. Secondly, the psychologist is increasingly being asked to make a constructive and practical contribution to the expanding area of moral education. Thirdly, the researcher is expected to demonstrate concern: in contrast with most other areas of psychology, in this field it is considered desirable to express a point of view and a commitment about the long-term effects of one's research.

In this chapter I am going to discuss a number of major issues in the psychology of moral development. I am not attempting a comprehensive review of the literature; several excellent reviews are available (Wright, 1971; Graham, 1972). At present, the term 'moral development' covers a number of aspects of development, growth and socialization, loosely linked by the diffuse, generic category 'moral'. The several theoretical approaches in the field do not only offer different interpretations of the data; they employ different definitions of morality. There is considerable fragmentation; the various aspects of moral development do not, on the whole, show much intercorrelation. The issues which I shall discuss reflect on the origins of this fragmentation, and on the implications for theory and for education.

Firstly, I shall look at different ways of defining 'morality', and consider how this affects the way in which psychologists approach moral socialization. Secondly, I shall consider the major theories and their concepts of development. Thirdly, I shall examine the ideas of 'character' and 'virtue', and the components of morality. Finally, I shall consider whether the evidence offers any possibility of a more integrated psychology of morality, and the implications of theory and data for educational practice.

The nature of morality

Social problems and moral engineering

The definition of morality depends very much on the orientation of the research under consideration. There are pressures on psychologists to explain, and provide recipes for the solution of, certain types of social problem. Considerable research attention has been paid to delinquency and violence. For the lay person, these social problems frequently have moral connotations. However there are few social scientists who would consider that large-scale violence can be accounted for by individual lack of impulse control. Not surprisingly, research on these issues has contributed considerably to an understanding of the cycle of deprivation and the effects of poor family relationships, but little to an understanding of moral development.

In the field of moral education, also, the psychologist is caught between lay and scientific definitions. Lay and traditional expectations of moral education are that it should inculcate discipline and, as Wright says, 'the control of unruly pupils and ... reduction of the incidence of theft, violence, vandalism and the like' (Wright, 1976). In fact, in Britain the role of the psychologist in moral education has been relatively minor to date. However as moral psychology becomes less eclectic and more cognition-oriented, psychologists are becoming more interested in education as 'the facilitation of new insights into moral problems, greater empathic awareness of others, are the growth of more mature cognitive structures' (Wright, 1976). The distinction, even conflict, between a 'vice and virtue' approach and a 'moral reasoning' approach is evident in theory as well as in practice, as will become apparent.

Major moral and ethical issues have been an important impetus to research. The events in Nazi Germany stimulated considerable research into the antecedents of evil (Adorno et al., 1950; Milgram, 1967). In the last decade, the American conscience has experienced many traumas, including the My Lai massacre and the Watergate affair, which between them include most of the major moral issues of Western culture. In addition to these negative moral experiences, there have been a number of positive ones, in particular, individual and collective resistance to oppression and injustice. Many psychologists writing about moral development cite these events, and express a commitment to developing an understanding of morality which might have a public effect. Many show optimism about being able to do so. Whether such a belief in the perfectibility of man is justified will have to be judged from the evidence. More specifically, however, there is a close relationship between the way that 'morality' is defined, and the kind of issue which is cited as a moral problem, as we shall see.

Conceptions of morality

Broadly, the psychologist has a choice of two definitions of morality within which to investigate development. The first is a normative, relativistic definition, which can loosely be called 'sociological'. According to this definition 'moral' acts, values or motives are those regarded as desirable or right by the society in which the individual lives. The basis of this view is that all cultures rear their children to conform to their code, and pass on from generation to generation the values and beliefs held. For the psychologist who adopts a normative definition, the interesting questions concern the means by which conformity to the norms is achieved through socialization of motives, and how values are transmitted across generations and internalized by the growing individuals.

The second definition might loosely be termed 'philosophical'. In a sense this is a meaningless label because three millenia of philosophical preoccupation with the nature of morality have produced a number of philosophical definitions of morality. However, those philosophers who have directly influenced the psychology of morality are united by certain common themes. The first of these is that the domain of 'moral' thought, action and motive can be distinguished from other domains. The second is that moral rules and principles are universal, or at least universalizable. The third is that there is a state or condition of 'moral maturity'; a person grows, at least potentially, to be able not only to generalize from the rule, but to generate new rules. For the psychologist who adopts this definition of morality, the interesting questions concern the growth of moral understanding.

There is a wide range of psychological theory within and between these approaches, and many psychologists use normative concepts to inform their philosophical-moral definitions, and vice versa. It would be a gross oversimplification, for example, to say that the social learning theory approach to moral development is exclusively normative, or that because character typology theorists and cognitive-developmental theorists both concentrate on the progressive development of 'morality', they are talking about the same thing. For the purpose of illustration it is useful to compare two theorists who in *some* ways exemplify each of the definitions. The first is Skinner, whose assumptions can be interpreted as ultra-normative. The second is Kohlberg, whose model is of 'the child as moral philosopher' (1968).

Skinner (1971) specifically denies many of the tenets of Western moral ideals by rejecting the concepts of autonomy and freedom. Skinner's argument is that a number of things follow logically from the scientific realization that everything about a human being's behaviour, values and motives is the consequence of contingencies of reinforcement. Firstly, there can be no freedom of choice, there can only be conflicts between contingencies of reinforcement; therefore education for moral choice is meaningless. Effective 'moral education' (socialization) would eliminate the possibility of choice between a 'good' and a 'bad' alternative, although there might remain some conflict between two equally 'good' alternatives. Secondly, that which is good is that which is reinforced, not vice versa. The only possible definition of 'good' is in these terms; having been reinforced for performing some action, we are then subsequently reinforced for *calling* it 'good', 'right' or 'moral', and these terms may subsequently act as continuing reinforcers for those actions because we learn that it is 'good' to be 'good'.

Thirdly, problems of anti-social behaviour and in fact all forms of 'immorality', including excesses of the appetites, are a consequence of incorrect reinforcement schedules. Therefore the solution to social problems, as well as to individual socialization, is to design a culture so that the contingencies of reinforcement are effective in ensuring the continued survival of the individual, the culture and ultimately the species.

Skinner's views are highly controversial, especially his utopian vision with its implied necessary component of 'psychologist kings' to design and control the schedules of reinforcement. For our present purposes, however, Skinner illustrates an extreme form of normative approach. This has a number of characteristics.

Firstly, moralization is not distinguishable from socialization. If being 'moral' equals being 'well socialized' then there is no psychological distinction between learning the moral rule and the mathematical rule, between learning to avoid being run over by cars and to avoid stealing. Secondly, the desired outcome of socialization is conformity to the rule and to the norm. Thirdly, the emphasis of socialization is on impulse control and the learning of the rule. Fourthly, the processes of socialization are processes of *acquisition* – of motives, values and behaviours – strengthened by practice and reinforcement.

Kohlberg (1964; 1969; 1970; 1976) concentrates solely on the development of moral reasoning. He rejects the 'bag of virtues' approach to morality on the grounds that the only acceptable definitions of morality concern ethics, not behaviour. Behaviour is neutral, morally, unless informed by ethical concepts. His research demonstrates the development of moral conceptualization through a series of stages. Kohlberg's approach to the development of morality is Kantian. The predominant theme of moral development is an understanding of justice, which comes to full fruition at stage 6. The definition of justice which Kohlberg employs is that of Rawls (1971). The stages are a succession of qualitative changes in moral 'ideology'; through development the child increases her understanding of relations between people, between the individual and the institution, and between rules and roles. In this process the child differentiates the various components of justice, and gradually integrates them.

Kohlberg has been criticized on several grounds. His emphasis on justice, to the exclusion of other aspects of morality such as concern for others, has been attacked as too limited (Peters, 1971; Puka, 1976). Orthodox empiricists have criticized his lack of interest in the behavioural correlates of moral reasoning (Kurtines and Greif, 1974). Several psychologists feel that, whatever the philosophical definition, psychology should take a more eclectic view of morality, with greater attention to practical issues and lay concepts. Kohlberg's theory is important in current thinking about moral development, so some of these criticisms will be considered in detail later. Here we will consider the contrast between Kohlberg and the normative approach.

Firstly, the conventional meaning of 'socialization' is not appropriate; Kohlberg argues that moral judgement development is not a matter of direct teaching. A cognitively stimulating environment, and socratic dialectical educational methods, may induce conflict and disequilibrium in the child, which may act as an impetus to further development, but moral judgement is not *learnt*. Secondly, the outcome of moral development is the capacity to make judgements on the basis of principle. Far from conforming, the individual may act in a disruptive way in accordance with these principles, for example to restore justice. Thirdly, the emphasis of socialization is on the encouragement of more differentiated and more integrated forms of reasoning and sociomoral comprehension. Fourthly, the focus is on *development*, not on acquisition. Moral *knowledge* is of course acquired, early in life, but the interesting questions concern how the rule is understood and justified. Development is via qualitative, not quantitative, changes in moral reasoning.

These two perspectives are theoretically consistent and systematic. In contrast, much research on moral development has been problem-centred or focused on one aspect of morality, and only fairly loosely linked to a specific theoretical approach. For most psychologists, the working definition of morality is a cluster of components: resistance to temptation, guilt, altruism, moral belief and moral insight. The origin of this cluster is cultural tradition; we have inherited a conception of the 'virtuous person', who possesses each of these components in good measure. In fact, psychological research has demonstrated very little correlation between these aspects of morality, but rather than modify the concept of the virtuous person, psychologists have concentrated on increasing the rigour of their investigation of the individual components.

The nature of the beast

All cultures have their model of the 'virtuous person', and employ various measures designed to produce a majority of such persons in every rising generation. Such a person knows the rules, and has acquired the motives which sustain her adherence to those rules. She herself contributes to general social control by judging her peers and operating shaming sanctions, or appeals to guilt, if they deviate. Ultimately, she will socialize those members of the next generation who are in her care.

Bronfenbrenner has illustrated the relationship between the cultural conception of the virtuous person and the socialization methods designed to produce her (Bronfenbrenner, 1962; Garbarino and

Bronfenbrenner, 1976). The cultural goal affects not only the content of socialization, but also its form. In Soviet society, following the teachings of Makarenko, the peer group is used extensively as the mediator of socialization, rather than direct adult authority. This reflects – and implements – the desired outcome of a collectivist morality. Parallels can be drawn with the kibbutz and other communally based societies.

Within our culture, the components and characteristics of the virtuous person are generally agreed, but there are considerable differences in assumptions about the inherent nature of man. The model of man affects the definition of morality and the conception of development. Is man passively moulded into virtue, or is virtue actively sought? Is man fundamentally evil, fundamentally good, or neither? Is virtue the triumph of reason over passion, or the triumph of good passion over evil passion? These are central questions, and different theories of moral development have different underlying assumptions.

Four distinct models can be detected in current approaches to moral development. In the first the infant is neither moral nor immoral at birth; she is devoid of motives, either pro- or anti-social. She is moulded and conditioned, and essentially passive. She acquires habits, motives and values, which may be pro- or anti-social. Temperamental variables may affect how easily she is conditioned, but conditioning also may modify some temperamental or innate tendencies.

In the second, in contrast, the infant is born with considerable potential for being anti-social. Development is a continual conflict between the pressures of the socializing environment, and the demands and desires of the individual. The lay version of this model places some emphasis on 'sin', and both lay and psychological models stress the importance of guilt and the development of impulse control.

The third model presumes that the individual is fundamentally good and would, if left alone, develop naturally into a virtuous person. The effect of society is largely corrupting. This viewpoint is usually attributed to Rousseau (1762). While it has few adherents within orthodox psychology, it has been influential in 'deschooling' educational movements and in some forms of progressive education (Neill, 1961). Kohlberg and Mayer (1972) link this model with psychoanalytically-based self-realization models as 'romantic' conceptions of man.

In the fourth model the individual actively seeks to understand the social world and to formulate rules for social intercourse. Virtue in this model is to a large extent equated with reason. The dominant issue of development is rational judgement rather than the growth of a sense of sin.

Theories of development

The three major theories of socialization, in their treatment of moral development, contain implicit models of man which affect how *development* is conceived. The implicit model also affects which aspects of morality are emphasized.

Social learning theory

Social learning theory has departed from the traditional behaviourism exemplified by Skinner in a number of significant ways, but it retains some of the assumptions. 'Socialization' is the acquisition of cultural values and the conditioning of moral anxiety, or conscience. The desired outcome of this is self-direction and impulse control by the individual, in ways appropriate to the culture. The emphasis of social learning theory is on the investigation of that which is observable, which predominantly means behaviour. Increasingly however there is a shift towards analysis of the intervening variables, and away from the contingencies of conditioning anxiety. The intervening variables include cognition, and the mechanisms of internalization (Aronfreed, 1968, 1976).

For some years the main focus of attention has been on modelling as the primary mechanism through which identification occurs. Modelling is a form of identification, though lacking many of the connotations which this concept has in psychoanalytic theory (see Graham, 1972). The child imitates the behaviour and the values of a significant other, because that person has characteristics which arouse a motive state in the child. The parent's love may be, or appear to be, contingent upon the child's good behaviour. Imitation in this context would have a dual function. The behaviour elicits direct approval from the parent, and by imitating the approving parent the child provides the basis for self-regulation. Her own acts, previously rewarded by the parent, can be reinforced when performed alone by her own imitative self-approval, 'Good girl!'. There is extensive evidence of the role of the modelling process in the acquisition of behaviour and values (Bandura and Walters, 1963; Berkowitz, 1964; Sears et al., 1965; Gewirtz, 1969).

Within the terminology of social learning theory conscience is conditioned anxiety, but there are a variety of ways in which this can be construed. At the most minimal level, conscience is anxiety which is conditioned classically to punishment, as demonstrated by the experiments of Solomon (1960, 1968). Solomon induced resistance to temptation and manifest anxiety ('guilt') in puppies. Eysenck (1976) argues that the only possible *scientific* theory of morality is in these terms. Like Skinner, he argues that 'immoral' or anti-social behaviour is caused by and can be dealt with by conditioning procedures and, as is widely known, he contends that biologically based differences in conditionability can account for failures of socialization.

Conscience is more liberally construed by other social learning theorists. Aronfreed (1976), for example, considers that there is a wide range of stimuli to which anxiety may be conditioned. He refers to these as 'monitors'. 'The precursors of a punished act may consist for example of behavioural cues which are produced by the child's own motoric orienting actions. But they may also take the far more interesting form of cognitive processes which range from the simplest representational images to the most complex evaluative structures (such as principles)' (p. 59).

Within its own terms of reference, social learning theory accounts adequately for the socialization of many aspects of social and moral behaviour. These terms emphasize the control, and self-control, of specific actions and habits, and the development of certain general dispositions and response tendencies – which might in another framework be termed 'virtues'.

Psychoanalytic theory

Traditional psychoanalytic theory emphasized the role of the superego in conscience development. With the resolution of the Oedipus complex a reservoir of guilt-energy was created from residual id energy, and concurrently parental values were introjected to form the ego-ideal (Freud, 1923). Latterday psychoanalytic writers have placed less emphasis on the development of the superego and the specific crisis at the age of five or six. Instead they have elaborated the integration typical of the ego, a process which involves balancing the destructive self-directed aggression of guilt against the love-oriented altruism directed towards others. Freud separated the judging function of the superego and the reasoning function of the ego. This implied a conflict relationship additional to the conflicts already existing between the id and other aspects of personality. Ego psychologists, however, regard the integration of the ego as the manifestation of full moral development (Gilligan, 1976; Loevinger, 1976).

In the terms of traditional theory, the anti-social and fantasy-based impulses of the individual, which equip her ill for survival in the social world, are channelled to reality and to the control of the self. The developmental process is conceived as conflict, between fantasy and reality, and between reason and passion. The role of guilt is problematic. Guilt is the internalized mechanism of control, and is essential therefore to the individual and to society; aggression turned in towards the self prevents aggression to others (Freud, 1930). Yet guilt inhibits happiness, and too much guilt creates neurosis. The oversocialized individual is not ego-balanced (Gilligan, 1976). The desirable outcome from the point of view of psychoanalytic theory, is the triumph of reason. Reason can resolve some of the conflicts, but reason is an ego function, and therefore, particularly in the terms of traditional theory, it cannot be free from conflict with id and superego influences.

The psychoanalytic analogue is unsatisfactory to many psychologists because it appears to be untestable. Many would prefer to argue that it is 'of historical interest only' – a generous euphemism. However, Freud has had a wide influence on our culture and on those grounds alone his conceptions of guilt and the dynamics of the sense of sin deserve to be given consideration. If nothing else, traditional psychoanalytic theory provides insight into why we think in terms of 'sin' and 'evil', rather in the more static terms of 'deviance' or 'lack of socialization'. To date no other approach in psychology has come to terms with the power of emotion associated with moral outrage, deep shame or existential guilt. The phenomena which are termed responses of the ego to threat, namely distortion of reality and of judgement, polarization of belief, and a rigid conviction of righteousness, are important and recognizable aspects of moral beliefs. The unsatisfactoriness of the developmental theory should not blind psychologists to the importance of the phenomenon.

Cognitive-developmental theory

Cognitive-developmental theory, the third perspective, will be treated more extensively, partly because of its rapidly growing importance and partly because, particularly in Britain, much of the material is relatively inaccessible. The main tenets of the approach have already been described; the emphasis on moral reasoning and the sense of justice, the conception of the child actively construing her world, with progressively greater differentiation and integration, and the progression through a series of qualitatively different stages of thought.

The originator of cognitive-developmental theory is of course Piaget. His work on the moral judgement of the child (1932) demonstrated three stages of moral thought in primary-school and pre-pubescent children; moral realism, morality of cooperation, and morality of equity. Although Piaget never integrated his cognitive and moral theories, the same principles and criteria of stage development can be applied in both. The stages are consistent internally – *structured wholes* – which form a hierarchy of successive progression, each stage integrating and consolidating the previous one (Pinard and Laurendeau, 1969; Flavell, 1971).

Kohlberg's work has considerably elaborated and extended many aspects of Piaget's model of moral development. His method, like Piaget's, presents the subject with four moral dilemmas which elicit moral reasoning. Kohlberg's stages are presented in Table 3.1. The claims of the stages to fulfil the criteria of cognitive-developmental theory have been established by experimental and by longitudinal studies. Kohlberg's original sample (1958) have been followed through into adulthood – the oldest subjects are now approaching forty (Kohlberg and Kramer, 1969; Kohlberg, 1973). Studies by Turiel (1966; 1969) and Rest (1969; 1973) have demonstrated that

Table 3.1   Moral stages

| Level and stage | Content of stage | |
	What is right	Reasons for doing right
LEVEL I: PRECONVENTIONAL Stage 1: Heteronomous morality	To avoid breaking rules backed by punishment, obedience for its own sake, and avoiding physical damage to persons and property.	Avoidance of punishment, and the superior power of authorities.
Stage 2: Individualism, instrumental purpose, and exchange	Following rules only when it is to someone's immediate interest; acting to meet one's own interests and needs and letting others do the same. Right is also what's fair, what's an equal exchange, a deal, an agreement.	To serve one's own needs or interests in a world where you have to recognize that other people have their interests too.

	Content of stage	
Level and stage	*What is right*	*Reasons for doing right*

LEVEL II: CONVENTIONAL

Stage 3: Multi inter-personal expectations, relationships, and interpersonal conformity | Living up to what is expected by people close to you or what people generally expect of people in your role as son, brother, friend, etc. 'Being good' is important and means having good motives, showing concern about others. It also means keeping mutual relationships, such as trust, loyalty, respect and gratitude. | The need to be a good person in your own eyes and those of others. Your caring for others. Belief in the Golden Rule. Desire to maintain rules and authority which support stereotypical good behaviour. |
| Stage 4: Social system and conscience | Fulfilling the actual duties to which you have agreed. Laws are to be upheld except in extreme cases where they conflict with other fixed social duties. Right is also contributing to society, the group, or institution. | To keep the institution going as a whole, to avoid the breakdown in the system 'if everyone did it', or the imperative of conscience to meet one's defined obligations. |

LEVEL III: POST-CONVENTIONAL or PRINCIPLED

| Stage 5: Social contract or utility and individual rights | Being aware that people hold a variety of values and opinions, that most values and rules are relative to your group. These relative rules should usually be upheld, however, in the interest of impartiality and because they are the social contract. Some non-relative values and rights like life and liberty, however, must be upheld in any society and regardless of majority opinion. | A sense of obligation to law because of one's social contract to make and abide by laws for the welfare of all and for the protection of all people's rights. A feeling of contractual commitment, freely entered upon, to family, friendship, trust, and work obligations. Concern that laws and duties be based on rational calculation of overall utility, 'the greatest good for the greatest number'. |
| Stage 6: Universal ethical principles | Following self-chosen ethical principles. Particular laws or social agreements are usually valid because they rest on such principles. When laws violate these principles one acts in accordance with the principle. Principles are universal principles of justice: the equality of human rights and respect for the dignity of human beings as individual persons. | The belief as a rational person in the validity of universal moral principles, and a sense of personal commitment to them. |

From Lickona (1976)

subjects reject the reasoning of earlier stages, and both prefer and comprehend best their current stage reasoning, and that of one stage above. Material of a higher stage is reinterpreted by the subject in terms of the reasoning of her own stage. Attempts to promote development – progression to the next stage – experimentally, using discussions, socratic methods and so forth, have demonstrated the difficulty of upsetting the existing structure of thinking except in the case of subjects who are already in transition (Lorimer, 1971; Blatt and Kohlberg, 1975).

These findings confirm that moral development is a slow process. In contrast with Piaget's conclusion, Kohlberg and others have shown that moral realism does not cease at the age of eight; it is still prevalent in ten-year-olds. The second stage of moral reasoning is found frequently in adults. Rational morality, in the sense of post-conventional reasoning, only begins to appear in late adolescence or in adulthood, and in any case it is very rare; studies of adult populations with above-average ability reveal a predominance of conventional reasoning (Haan, Smith and Block, 1968; Fontana and Noel, 1973).

As noted earlier, Kohlberg argues that the evidence supports a definition of morality based on the principle of justice (1971). In his view, justice is the only moral principle which (a) subsumes other aspects of morality, and (b) in the course of development passes through and subsequently transcends both conventional and utilitarian-contractual reasoning. He sees the stages as increasingly sophisticated conceptions of justice. They demonstrate awareness of increasingly complex equity, and a growing understanding of the variables necessarily to be considered in making a just judgement. Until the final stage, the individual is, as it were, juggling with these variables, in each stage in an increasingly complex manner. At the final stage there comes the full realization that only the principle itself can be the basis for judgement.

Studies of the correlates of moral reasoning development provide a basis for assessing Kohlberg's claims for the greater moral adequacy of the later stages, and the primacy of the principle of justice. First, let us consider the relationship between moral judgement and moral action. There is little evidence that conventionally 'moral' behaviour relates *directly* to moral reasoning. A possible exception to this is a finding by Thornton (1977) that the *type* of crime committed was related to stage of moral reasoning. On the whole, where a relationship exists, there is ample evidence of a third variable intervening. Usually this is intelligence, which correlates highly with moral reasoning. Delinquents show immature moral reasoning but they show other characteristics as well (Kohlberg, 1958; Hudgins and Prentice, 1973). Kohlberg urges that ego-strength and other forms of personal competence intervene between moral judgement and impulse control (Kohlberg, 1963; Grim, Kohlberg and White, 1968).

In contrast, there is a definite relationship between moral judgement and what might be termed action performed in the service of an ideological belief or principle. Subjects with post-conventional reasoning were likely to resist an experimenter's pressure to inflict pain on subjects (Milgram, 1965; McNamee, 1977). Post-conventional students and faculty were much more likely than conventional ones to be involved in disruptive activities protesting against what they regarded as unethical tactics of institutions (Haan et al., 1968; Fishkin, Keniston and McKinnon, 1973). Stage 2 students (but not faculty) were also involved in protest; in their case, it seems that their moral outrage was less a matter of ethics, more a reaction to unfairness conceived in concrete terms of 'we' and 'they'.

It would seem from this evidence that moral judgement mediates action which *intervenes in the social process*, rather than acting as a control on personal impulse. There is some evidence, however, that the link between personal morality and moral judgement is through guilt. The description of subjective guilt reflects the general orientation of the dominant stage; for example, stage 2 subjects describe it as a fear of being caught, stage 4 subjects as an *alter ego*, judging the self (Weinreich, 1970).

A second correlate of moral reasoning is role-taking ability. 'Role-taking' is a rather confused concept which has been used to refer to anything from an empathic response to a simple perceptual capacity. For many people, empathy is a central concept of morality and, as we shall see later, there is some debate as to whether empathy is the consequence of moral development or one of its origins. Piaget defined role-taking as the capacity to see the other's point of view, and regarded it as a prerequisite for movement into the second stage. He also argued that it developed as a consequence of peer interaction. Subsequent attempts to relate peer interaction and moral stage have not been particularly successful (Kohlberg, 1958). Latterly, however, Selman (1976) has developed a satisfactory measure of *social perspective taking*. Stages of social perspective taking parallel, and are *prerequisites* for, the development of moral stages (see Table 3.2).

Table 3.2   Selman's stages of social perspective-taking

I *Egocentric point of view.* Doesn't consider the interests of others or recognize that they differ from the actor's; doesn't relate two points of view. Actions are considered physically rather than in terms of psychological interests of others. Confusion of authority's perspective with one's own.	**II** *Concrete individualistic perspective.* Aware that everybody has his own interest to pursue and these conflict, so that right is relative (in the concrete individualistic sense).
III *Perspective of the individual in relationships with other individuals.* Aware of shared feelings, agreements, and expectations which take primacy over individual interests. Relates points of view through the concrete. Golden Rule, putting yourself in the other guy's shoes. Does not yet consider generalized system perspective.	**IV** *Differentiates societal point of view from interpersonal agreement or motives.* Takes the point of view of the system that defines roles and rules. Considers individual relations in terms of place in the system.
V *Prior-to-society perspective.* Perspective of a rational individual aware of values and rights prior to social attachments and contracts. Integrates perspectives by formal mechanisms of agreement contract, objective impartiality, and due process. Consider moral and legal points of view; recognizes that they sometimes conflict and finds it difficult to integrate them.	**VI** *Perspective of a moral point of view* from which social arrangements derive. Perspective is that of any rational individual recognizing the nature of morality or the fact that persons are ends in themselves and must be treated as such.

From Lickona (1976)

A third correlate of moral reasoning is cognitive development. This does not directly affect the claims of greater *moral* adequacy of the later stages, but there are some implications for the way the stages are seen as a total system. Several studies indicate that formal operations are a necessary (but not sufficient) condition for proper transition from stage 3 to stage 4 (Kuhn, Langer, Kohlberg and Haan, 1972; Cauble, 1976). Less clear evidence suggests that stage 2, but not stage 1, requires concrete operations. Traditionally, the stages have been linked in pairs to form levels, on the basis of the dominant content themes. The evidence of related cognitive function suggests that the levels may be misleading. Changing the grouping of the stages would have little effect on the view that justice is the primary issue. On the other hand it would make *possible* an alternative interpretation. This is that the first three stages represent progress from an authority-based morality, through a morality of expediency and utility, to a morality of humanity and compassion. The second three stages *repeat* this cycle, at an *abstract* level. A form of this view is that the final three stages are *parallel* forms of abstract moral reasoning, not sequential (e.g. Gibbs, 1977).

Kohlberg's theory has been widely accepted, especially in the United States. The particular appeal seems to be on two counts: firstly the emphasis on cognition, secondly the fact that it is a developmental theory. There has been in psychology an increasing interest in cognition and information processing, and a movement towards a more active model of man. Developmental theory implies a theory of progress, a shift away from deterministic models which concentrate on acquisition mediated by the social environment. Sullivan (1977) also argues that the theory has particular appeal to contemporary culture: 'In a culture deeply involved in moral problems related to race, poverty and war, this theory offered a concept of justice which promised to deal with the quagmire of value relativity.'

Not everyone is enthusiastic, however. The emphasis on justice, despite its honourable Kantian tradition, is to many people too limiting as a definitional criterion of morality. There is still an unresolved issue, as to whether the concept of justice is in fact necessary for the *developmental* theory (as opposed to the *moral* theory). Redefinitions like that of Gibbs cited above, suggest that the developmental theory could operate with a different core emphasis. Could not cognitions be about compassion rather than about justice?

Finally, there are reservations about the empirical status of the theory. While the earlier stages are well-documented by cross-age samples, and by longitudinal studies, post-conventional thought is rare and the number of its examples small. This creates difficulties especially in view of the importance of post-conventional thought to the definitional base of the theory. It is not helped either by Kohlberg's recent (1977) re-analysis of stages 5 and 6 (Kurtines and Greif, 1974; Trainer, 1977).

'Character' and 'virtue'

The theories outlined above, particularly social learning and cognitive-developmental theory, focus very specifically and in depth on certain aspects and conceptions of morality, ignoring others. Neither theory makes any attempt to incorporate traditional conceptions of 'character'. There are historical reasons why 'character' has apparently not survived psychological analysis.

Character traditionally has two meanings. One encompasses the concept of the virtuous person; a collection of moral traits with the assumption of predictability between them. The other means adherence to a higher-order principle, which implies strength of will as well as a grasp of the principle. The demolition of the trait model occurred early in the history of research. Hartshorne and May (1928–30), as is well known, found low correlations between honesty and other moral traits. Their findings have been highly influential in the argument that many 'virtues' and traits are situation-specific, and mutually independent. In fact, subsequent re-analysis of their data (Brogden, 1940; Eysenck, 1953; Burton, 1963) produced some evidence of a common 'moral' factor, and Mackinnon (1938) did find interpredictability from one aspect of morality to another, but with an adult sample.

The problem may be partly methodological. Many studies of moral traits are conducted in laboratories, frequently with trivial tasks, which may evoke more situational than moral variables. Quasi-naturalistic studies by Milgram (1963; 1965) and by Zimbardo (1974) demonstrated that the situation can wreak havoc with character and virtue, when the pressures are against, rather than towards, 'moral' action. (Zimbardo and his associates ran a prison simulation with students, and were disturbed to find how rapidly the actors degenerated into their roles.)

'Developmental character typologies' exist in various forms and have a long history. They have tended to present a mixed bag, not only of virtues, but of reasoning, values, and motives. However, even if supported by empirical studies, they offer little. Their common theme is that development progresses from anarchy, through authority-based and then peer-based sanctions, until the final state of autonomy is achieved. Ostensibly, all aspects of morality are integrated in the process. Theoretically, these models are eclectic. Because they lack rigour, they cannot be called 'stage' theories.

Wright (1971) has summarized the character typologies diagram-
matically. (see Figure 3.1). The hierarchy reflects an *evaluation*, regarding the degree of moral sophistication of the type. It does not
necessarily follow that there is only one route to moral autonomy. The
problem with these typologies is that there is insufficient empirical
data to substantiate them. The cost of their eclecticism is a lack of
definitional clarity. The question of transition from one type to the
'next', is not dealt with, and the supposed interrelationship between
the various aspects of morality is taken for granted, without analysis.
While there may be strong arguments in favour of attempting to
integrate, the character typologies in existence are too speculative, and
too reliant on an unquestioning acceptance of lay assumptions, to be
equipped to come to terms with the difficult conceptual issues
involved.

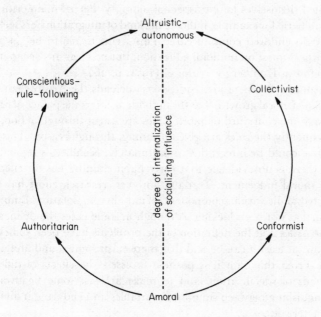

Mainly adult influence ----------------------------- Mainly peer influence

Fig. 3.1 Diagrammatic summary of character typologies (Wright, 1971)
based on material from McDougall (1908); Swainson (1949); Havighurst and
Taba (1949); Peck and Havighurst (1960) *inter alia*.

But there are many who defend a pluralistic conception of morality, despite the problems of the psychological evidence. Hogan (1973) proposed a five-dimensional model of moral character, deriving from man's 'natural' rule-following and rule-formulating tendencies. These dimensions are moral knowledge, socialization, empathy, autonomy, and moral judgement. They are sequential phases of development, which interact with one another and influence both conduct and perception. (Hogan's model resembles the character typologists, but differs from them in the rigour of its conceptualization and experimentation.) Peters (1971) defends virtue as a necessary addition to any rational model of moral development.

These writers are seeking to define morality in a way which integrates philosophical and psychological considerations. They are not asking the same *kind* of questions as those psychologists who, accepting the implications of the Hartshorne and May study, have devoted themselves to one aspect of morality. Peters' main criticisms of Kohlberg, for example, indicate the kind of integration he is seeking. 'How do children come to care? This seems to me to be the most important question in moral education; but no clear answer to it can be found in Kohlberg's writings.' (1971, p. 262)

Secondly, Peters (1963; 1971; 1974) defends the Aristotelian conception of moral growth, that the individual enters the palace of reason through the courtyard of habit. Rules are learnt through action, and subsequently the rules are given meaning, through reason. This perspective could be integrative; unfortunately, Kohlberg's rejoinder is that there is no evidence that early habit-training has an effect on later moral judgement. To date, however, research effort has been directed to the various components of morality, in isolation. Empirical rigour has not been lacking. Although in some cases the delineation of the issues and the definition of the problems have been somewhat narrow, at least it can be said that there exists some sound and useful data. From this data it is possible to assess the effects of different methods of socialization, and to make at least some headway in distinguishing between situational variables and enduring individual characteristics.

The components of morality

Altruism

Of all the components of morality, altruism has been the least amenable to analysis. It has tended to be seen as an extension of empathy, yet the research data consistently seems to indicate strong situational dependence. In part, the difficulty is to define what is to be explained. Many of the characteristics which come under this heading are general traits or qualities; people are *expected* to be helpful, sympathetic and so forth, and selfishness is not usually regarded as a *moral* failing. Altruism concerns the extremes. Apart from obvious acts of heroism, at the positive end there are forms of good samaritanism, going out of one's way, being self-sacrificing for the benefit of another. The negative aspect is exemplified by the case of Kitty Genovese, who was murdered in front of thirty-eight witnesses. This event created the same degree of moral outrage and impetus to research among psychologists as the other traumas mentioned at the beginning of the chapter.

Explanation of altruism is complicated by the basic assumptions of most psychological theories, that man is inherently selfish and hedonistic. Rosenhan (1969; 1972) has found a kind of solution in social learning theory terms. Either the gratitude or other positive affect of the recipient of altruism is rewarding, or alternatively the child develops a response tendency as a consequence of receiving approval from parents for the performance of altruistic acts. This theory however builds in a concept of self-reward, which rather diminishes the usual definition of altruism.

Psychoanalytic theory has been cynical about altruism; altruistic behaviour is the symptom of inner conflicts, and the manifestation of a desire for domination or manipulation, or a projection of one's needs on to others.

A less pessimistic interpretation is provided by a theory which does not otherwise contribute to moral psychology. This is equity theory, a cognitive social theory, on Lewinian principles, which accounts for interpretations of the social situation (Walster and Piliavin, 1972). A sense of imbalance is created in the bystander by the perception of differential equity, e.g. by an injured person or a victim. The bystander can rectify this inequality either by helping, or by distorting the situation (diminishing its seriousness), denying her responsibility, or degrading the victim. The advantage of equity theory is that it accounts for various possible reactions in social-psychological rather than in moral terms.

There persists, however, a view that altruism must relate to empathy. The distinction has already been made between approaches which regard empathy as the manifestation of moral maturity, and those which regard empathy as a prime force in impelling development. Ego psychologists, for example, regard altruism as part of the ego process; the self depends upon the altruism of others, and can achieve its fullest expression only in social interaction. Altruism is therefore regarded as a consequence of ego integration (Katz, 1972).

The correlates of altruism do not support a personality or trait model. The data on the whole suggest situational determinants (Wispé, 1972). Huston and Korte (1976) argue that there is a 'good samaritan' profile, which consists of a constellation of values or world view rather than motives or traits. Cognitive-based variables are important; we have already noted the relationship between moral reasoning levels and certain types of helping behaviour under difficult conditions (Milgram, 1967; McNamee, 1977). Schwartz (1968) found that people who regard themselves as responsible for the welfare of others are more likely to show helpfulness under emergency conditions. Overall the findings consistently show that a general *competence*, including cognitive competence, are significant variables in altruism. We shall return to competence later.

Resistance to temptation

Resistance to temptation is for many people *the* central issue of morality. Partly this is because effective resistance to temptation has been regarded as a valid criterion of internalization. Partly however it arises from the traditional combination of Protestant values, in which pleasure is regarded with suspicion, and resistance to the temptations of the flesh and of the spirit is the mark of the godly.

There are two ways of looking at the origins of resistance to temptation. One, the more simplistic, is to treat it simply as the result of effective anxiety conditioning. The tempting stimulus becomes the CS, eliciting the CR, guilt (or avoidance behaviour). Another, more complex, approach argues that resistance to temptation is part of a wider response style, and is not purely a moral phenomenon. Grim, Kohlberg and White (1968), for example, found that the best predictor of resistance to temptation was span of attention. Mischel and Mischel (1976) report a series of their own studies which demonstrate the relationship between a capacity to delay gratification in general, and resistance to temptation and self-control. Their argument is that resistance to temptation, and self-regulation in general, is part of *competence*. 'Competence' includes a wide range of intellectual and cognitive functions, including life-planning, of which 'moral' characteristics are necessarily a part. We saw above that competence is an important associated variable of altruism also.

Guilt

The importance of guilt to the theory of socialization has already been discussed. A central issue for psychologists has been to establish the antecedents of guilt. However, guilt has many meanings.

One meaning of guilt is *pre-transgression anxiety*. Ostensibly, this operates as an inhibitor; its measured strength should in some sense be an indication of the probability of the performance of unacceptable action. Another meaning of guilt is *post-transgression anxiety*. This takes a number of forms, for example confession, restitution, remorse, and intrapunitive behaviour. As it obviously is not concerned with the effective control of behaviour, its operation has a different interest. It is a motive state; usually it has been treated as an indicator of the extent of the individual's guilt – that is, as an indirect measure of the success of internalization (Johnson, Dockecki and Mowrer, 1972). However, as a motive state, it is likely to affect perceptions of the situation. Wright (1971) has argued that the cognitive-dissonance aspects of post-transgression anxiety have been ignored. What is the relationship between the extent of post-transgression anxiety, for example, and the perceived magnitude of the sin? There are interest-in questions regarding the way in which atonement or post-hoc justifications operate as means of adjusting or overcoming the anxiety.

A further aspect, or perhaps an analogue, of guilt is shame. Several writers have suggested that the emphasis on guilt may be ethnocentric. (Ausubel, 1955; Gilligan, 1976). Benedict (1946) distinguished between 'guilt' cultures and 'shame' cultures. The former instil controls through the development of intrapunitive aggression, the latter through the force of public disapproval, or extrapunitive aggression. This distinction creates problems for Western psychologists, because shame is regarded as a less developed form of anxiety than guilt; most developmental theories postulate a stage or form of shame-based morality, through which the individual passes before the full internalization of guilt. Benedict however argues that 'in the United States we do not expect shame to do the heavy work of morality. We do not harness the acute personal chagrin which accompanies shame to our fundamental system of morality'.

This illustrates some of the possible limitations of our conception of guilt. We assume that shame and guilt operate in different ways. Shame is the judgement by others for failure to uphold the social code; it is not necessarily only concerned with moral issues. Guilt implies a sense of sin, it is exclusively a moral category, and concerns judgement by the self, not others. Yet as has been noted, many people describe their sense of guilt in terms of the *implied* judgement of others. Ausubel (1955) considers that the distinction is too pure to be useful psychologically. Shame and guilt operate in all cultures; shame cultures classify as 'shame' much that in American culture would be called guilt, and guilt cultures define 'shame' in terms of guilt. This resolution retains the developmental relationship between shame and guilt, but alerts us to the confusions arising from an idealization of guilt.

Finally, it is generally held that guilt is not enough. The 'morally mature' individual transcends guilt, particularly irrational-conscientious guilt, and becomes 'autonomous' or at least develops 'existential guilt'. These terms cover a variety of conceptions, but there is considerable evidence that there is a valid concept of a morality not governed solely by protestant-ethic anxiety.

The antecedents of conscience

Hoffman's studies on the antecedents of morality indicate that there are three types of conscience, and there is a definite relationship between the type of conscience and parental socialization methods (1963; 1970; Hoffman and Salzstein, 1967).

The first type of conscience is characterized by punishment anxiety, which *may* operate as a deterrent to action, but is equally likely to be evoked only after transgression. The second type of conscience is characterized by fear of loss of love. This has powerful guilt force, effective in maintaining what Hoffman (and others) call a 'conventional' morality. Both these types of guilt rest upon anxiety about the consequences of transgression to the *actor*. Hoffman distinguishes a third type of conscience characterized by 'existential' or 'ontological' guilt. Such guilt is directed to the effects of actions upon others rather than upon the self. It is an empathic rather than an intrapunitive form of guilt. Hoffman calls this type of conscience a 'humanistic' morality.

He studied the effects of power assertive, love withdrawal and induction (reasoning about the consequences of action) techniques of child-rearing. On various measures of guilt and other moral responses, the induction technique emerged as clearly superior. In contrast, power assertive methods actually had *negative* effects. Love withdrawal was more associated with the development of conventional morality, and induction with the development of humanistic morality. Hoffman came to five conclusions, which provide a succinct summary of the process of interaction between child-rearing practices and conscience development.

(1) Power assertion generates anger in the child and also provides the child with a model for the expression of anger.

(2) All techniques of discipline imply parental disapproval, and therefore arouse the child's need for approval. Love withdrawal techniques increase this anxiety; induction techniques diminish this anxiety because disapproval is only part of the process of induction, and the reasoning process gives a *justification* for the disapproval.

(3) Power assertive and love withdrawal techniques focus both affect and attention on the actor, whereas induction techniques focus on the effects of actions upon others.

(4) Expectations are built up in the child, based on previous experience of discipline techniques; therefore the child will interpret a particular act of discipline in terms of the prevalent mode to which she is accustomed. (Whilst I was writing this, Benny Green told an apposite anecdote of a music critic who reported admonishing his nagging son thus: '"Shut up!" I explained.')

(5) Effective techniques are those which enlist existing emotional and motivational resources within the child. Obviously the need for parental approval is essential for the acquisition of guilt.

Hoffman contends that *empathy* is important. He does not regard it as something which is acquired, but as a *natural proclivity*, elicited by appropriate (inductive) techniques. Empathy then becomes a motive force in its own right on which further moral socialization can develop (Hoffman, 1976).

Some studies of the correlates of moral reasoning substantiate Hoffman's conclusions. The relationship between moral reasoning and political action was discussed earlier. These studies also demonstrated a relationship between moral stage and the evaluation of desirable personal characteristics, and between moral stage and reported parental socialization techniques (Haan et al., 1968). Stage 5 and stage 6 subjects reported parents who were not particularly expressive, but were concerned with respect for individual rights. These parents were seen as actively involved with their children, and as conflict-inducing. Conventional – stage 3 and stage 4 – subjects, in contrast, reported relatively conflict-free relations with their parents, clear rules, and clear expectations of good behaviour. Parents used privileges as a means of encouragement and of discipline.'

All these findings pose something of a theoretical problem. In the case of the moral reasoning studies, it is explicit that a developmental sequence is involved. It is not clear whether Hoffman regards his types of conscience as forming a developmental sequence, but much of what he says implies that they are treated as such. The conventional approach of seeking antecedent conditions is a means of accounting for individual or group differences; it assumes that the antecedent conditions determine the *type*. This kind of exercise would therefore only be meaningful in this situation if the stages manifested among these students can be regarded as *terminal*: if the question we are asking is, what are the antecedent conditions which prevent people progressing beyond stage 3 or 4, or whatever. If we assume that these subjects are en route to further development, then we can only ask the weaker question, why are these subjects developing more slowly.

Implications

Moral education

What are the implications of the issues and evidence discussed above for moral education? The increasing emphasis on cognition, and on development rather than on acquisition, has highlighted the importance of the period of adolescence in moral growth. Acquisition models, in contrast, emphasize the significance of early childhood. The existing evidence, however, continues to stress the role of parents in fostering development, rather than the school. Some points, by no means exhaustive, can be drawn from the foregoing discussions.

Firstly, it remains a matter of debate as to whether any form of *virtues* can be taught in the school situation. As we have seen Kohlberg strongly attacks such a concept of moral education, partly on the grounds of its ineffectiveness. Other writers (e.g. Sugarman, 1973) argue that the school does have some influence on what might be termed virtues or response tendencies, if only because the child spends a great deal of time, and is exposed to a wide variety of influences, information and interactions at school. The strongest conclusion that can be made, given both theory and evidence, is that the school has prevailing *norms*, of behaviour and values, which are likely to have an effect over time. This includes, of course, both official and unofficial norms.

One way in which the school can be effective is by the provision of a 'just community' (Kohlberg, 1970; Fenton, 1976). In such a community, the primary principle, justice, is practised in such a way that every member of the community is involved. In such an environment, the child can be constantly exposed to moral discussion as well. While such a community demands quite radical changes in the school system, it has at least the merit of being demonstrably successful. The evidence, however, has more specific relevance to the micro-situation of teaching, the class contact between teacher and pupils, and most particularly to moral reasoning. The emphasis on cognitive aspects of morality (not only reasoning) and on the importance of cognitive stimulation in the developmental process, gives teachers scope for intervention. The danger is, however, that this may be interpreted as being an effective way to produce principled morality. A proper interpretation of the data is more pessimistic.

Socratic methods and discussions in which children are exposed to the arguments of a higher moral stage are effective in stimulating movement to the next stage *only* if the individual is already on the way towards transition. The process of consolidation and integration of a stage of moral thought is slow and complex; only up to a point can it be accelerated. The advantages of conflictual discussion and the stimulation of questioning is that it leads to what the Americans call 'values clarification' a process which itself promotes change. While it is, therefore, unlikely that such a programme of moral education will produce many more post-conventional sixth-formers, it is likely to produce stage 3 fourth-formers with a livelier awareness of the issues and of alternative interpretations of them.

What are the implications for dealing with specific issues? The main conclusion of all studies is that the individual reinterprets whatever is presented in terms of her own stage of thought, and that material that is, or appears to be, couched in terms of a lower stage is rejected. Hampden-Turner and Whitten (1971) argue that one of the problems arising from this is that the stage 4 person may reject a stage 6 argument partly because it *sounds like* a stage 2 argument, given that the subtleties of stage 6 reasoning elude her. Therefore, whether the teacher's aim is to increase consideration for others, or to counter the arguments of the National Front, the message of the data is clear; she must present a basis for discussion within the parameters of the stage appropriate to that at which the children are currently operating.

The state of psychological theory

The weight of the evidence reviewed in this chapter supports the general direction in which theory is going, towards an increasing emphasis on cognitive rather than on personality processes. This is not only an emphasis on reasoning; there is increased recognition of the role that rational process and cognition play in other aspects of morality (Ausubel, 1971).

Secondly, the concept of development is undergoing revision and clarification. Increasingly the evidence is in favour of morality *developing*, not being acquired as a consequence of teaching or training. Undoubtedly certain aspects of morality are acquired, for example basic moral knowledge, and specific forms of guilt anxiety, but this is a *basis*. There is constant change and modification taking place throughout childhood and adolescence.

Thirdly, trait models have been shown to be unsatisfactory. While many 'moral traits' or, in Peters' terminology, 'virtues' are desirable in their own right and merit fostering in the child, their relationship to other aspects of morality seems to be tenuous. On the whole, virtues are endstates; they do not seem to be an impetus to further moral growth or to the integration of morality. A possible exception is empathy, which, as has been noted, is regarded by some writers as a catalyst for growth and development. Increasingly, however, as the definitions become less confused and the investigations more rigorous, it appears that it is the more cognitive elements of empathy which are important in development.

The consistent finding which emerges is the relationship between many facets of morality, and *competence* of various kinds. Competence implies effectiveness, personality integration, ego strength and the capacity for life planning. Indirect support for this trend is provided by the evidence that the child-rearing practices which appear to be conducive to the development of the 'morally mature' person are also those associated with the production of competence (Baumrind, 1967, 1972).

Mischel and Mischel (1976) have developed a model which deals with a specific definition of competence. In their 'cognitive social learning' approach they attempt to integrate moral judgement, moral conduct and self-regulation. In this model, there are two moral components: the individual's *competence* to generate pro-social behaviours, and the motivational variables effecting the *performance* of these behaviours. This model allows for the separate analysis of the two components, in addition to providing a basis for theoretical integration. 'Competence' in this sense includes the active organization of information, and is closely related to intelligence and to intellectual functioning. Moral reasoning is in many ways that sort of function, with a particular and specialist area of discourse, and with affective elements to be included in the organization.

Mischel and Mischel's analysis of moral stages as a competence function is, potentially, a possible way of bridging the gap between thought and action which has always been a problem in moral psychology. Furthermore, there is a wide range of overlap between moral and other activities associated with appraisal, both of the self and of the environment. If treating moral reasoning as a competence function is a way of integrating these theoretically, it is possibly a first step to bridging the gap between the definition of 'moral' derived from philosophical bases, and the more diffuse operational definitions of morality which have been prevalent in psychological studies.

Finally, the boundaries of the definition of 'moral' are changing, particularly in the context of moral reasoning. The now well-established relationships between moral, political and social reasoning, and the overlap with cognition and also with ego processes are provocative (Kohlberg and Gilligan, 1971; Podd, 1972; Candee, 1974; Haan, Stroud and Holstein, 1973; Weinreich, 1974, 1977). To date, these have been explained in terms of one form of development being separate from another but a prerequisite for it (Kohlberg et al., 1977). In the writer's view, there is sufficient evidence to suggest that more is going on in this area of development than the present models, and the present definitions of morality, can fully account for.

References

Adorno, T. W., Frenkel-Brunswik, E., Levinson, D. J. and Sanford, R. N. (1950) *The Authoritarian Personality*. New York: Harper.

Aronfreed, J. (1968) *Conduct and Conscience: The Socialization of Internalized Control over Behaviour*. New York: Academic Press.

Aronfreed, J. (1976) Moral development from the standpoint of a general psychological theory. In T. Lickona (ed.) *Moral Development and Behaviour*. New York: Holt, Rinehart and Winston.

Ausubel, D. P. (1955) Relationships between shame and guilt in the socializing process. *Psychological Review 62*: 378–90.

Ausubel, D. P. (1971) Psychology's undervaluation of the rational components in moral behaviour. In C. M. Beck, B. S. Crittenden and E. V. Sullivan (eds) *Moral Education: Interdisciplinary Approaches*. Toronto: University of Toronto Press.

Bandura, A. and Walters, R. M. (1963) *Social Learning and Personality Development*. New York: Holt, Rinehart and Winston.

Baumrind, D. (1972) From each according to her ability. *School Review 80*: 161–97.

Baumrind, D. and Black, A. (1967) Socialization practices associated with dimensions of competence in pre-school boys and girls. *Child Development 38*: 291–327.

Benedict, R. (1946) *The Chrysanthemum and the Sword*. Boston: Houghton-Mifflin.

Berkowitz, L. (1964) *The Development of Motives and Values in the Child*. New York: Basic Books.

Blatt, M. M. and Kohlberg, L. (1975) The effects of classroom moral discussion upon children's level of moral judgement. *Journal of Moral Education 4*: 129–61.

Brogden, H. E. (1940) A factor analysis of forty character traits. *Psychological Monographs 52*: 39–55.

Bronfenbrenner, U. (1962) Soviet methods of character education. *American Psychologist 17*: 550–64.

Burton, R. V. (1963) Generality of honesty reconsidered. *Psychological Review 70*: 481–99.

Candee, D. (1974) Ego developmental aspects of New Left ideology. *Journal of Personality and Social Psychology 30*: 620–30.

Cauble, M. A. (1976) Formal operations, ego identity and principled morality: are they related? *Development Psychology 12*: 363–4.

Eysenck, H. J. (1953) *The Structure of Human Personality*. London: Methuen.

Eysenck, H. J. (1976) The biology of morality. In T. Lickona (ed.) *Moral Development and Behaviour*. New York: Holt, Rinehart and Winston.

Fenton, E. (ed.) (1976) Cognitive-developmental approach to moral education. *Social Education 40* (4, whole).

Fishkin, J., Keniston, K. and McKinnon, C. (1973) Moral reasoning and political ideology. *Journal of Personality and Social Psychology 27*: 109–19.

Flavell, J. (1971) Stage-related properties of cognitive development. *Cognitive Psychology 2*: 421–53.

Fontana, A. F. and Noel, B. (1973) Moral reasoning in the university. *Journal of Personality and Social Psychology 27*: 419–29.

Freud, S. (1923) *The Ego and the Id*. London: Hogarth Press/International Psychoanalytic Library.

Freud, S. (1930) *Civilization and its Discontents*. London: Hogarth Press/ International Psychoanalytic Library.

Garbarino, J. and Bronfenbrenner, U. (1976) The socialization of moral judgement and behaviour in cross-cultural perspective. In T. Lickona (ed.) *Moral Development and Behaviour*. New York: Holt, Rinehart and Winston.

Gewirtz, J. L. (1969) Mechanisms of social learning: some roles of stimulation and behaviour in early human development. In D. A. Goslin (ed.) *Handbook of Socialization Theory and Research*. Chicago: Rand McNally.

Gibbs, J. C. (1977) Kohlberg's stages of moral judgement: a constructive critique. *Harvard Educational Review* 47: 43–61.

Gilligan, J. (1976) Beyond morality: psychoanalytic reflections on shame, guilt and love. In T. Lickona (ed.) *Moral Development and Moral Behaviour*. New York: Holt, Rinehart and Winston.

Graham, D. (1972) *Moral Learning and Development*. London: Batsford.

Grim, P. F., Kohlberg, L. and White, S. H. (1968) Some relationships between conscience and attentional processes. *Journal of Personality and Social Psychology* 8: 239–52.

Haan, N., Smith, M. B. and Block, J. (1968) Moral reasoning of young adults. *Journal of Personality and Social Psychology* 10: 183–201.

Haan, N., Stroud, J. and Holstein, C. (1973) Moral and ego stages in relationship to ego processes: a study of 'hippies'. *Journal of Personality* 41: 596–612.

Hampden-Turner, C. and Whitten, P. (1971) Morals left and right. *Psychology Today* (US) 4 (11): 39–43, 74–6.

Hartshorne, H. and May, M. A. (1928–30) *Studies in the Nature of Character*. New York: Macmillan.

Havighurst, R. J. and Taba, H. (1949) *Adolescent Character and Personality*. New York: Wiley.

Hoffman, M. L. (1973) Child rearing practices and moral development: generalizations from empirical research. *Child Development* 34: 295–318.

Hoffman, M. L. (1970) Conscience, personality and socialization techniques. *Human Development* 13: 90–126.

Hoffman, M. L. (1976) Empathy, role-taking, guilt and development of altruistic motives. In T. Lickona (ed.) *Moral Development and Behaviour*. New York: Holt, Rinehart and Winston.

Hoffman, M. L. and Saltzstein, H. D. (1967) Parent discipline and the child's moral development. *Journal of Personality and Social Psychology* 5: 45–7.

Hogan, R. (1973) Moral conduct and moral character. A psychological perspective. *Psychological Bulletin* 79: 217–32.

Hudgins, W. and Prentice, N. M. (1973) Moral judgement in delinquent and non-delinquent adolescents and their mothers. *Journal of Abnormal Psychology* 82: 145–52.

Huston, T. L. and Korte, C. (1976) The responsive bystander: why he helps. In T. Lickona (ed.) *Moral Development and Behaviour*. New York: Holt, Rinehart and Winston.

Johnson, R. C., Dokecki, P. R. and Mowrer, O. H. (1972) *Conscience, Contract and Social Reality*. New York: Holt, Rinehart and Winston.

Katz, J. (1972) Altruism and sympathy: their history in philosophy and some implications for psychology. *Journal of Social Issues* 28: 59–69.

Kay, W. (1968) *Moral Development*. London: George Allen and Unwin.

Kohlberg, L. (1958) The development of modes of moral thinking and choice in the years ten to sixteen. Unpublished Ph.D. thesis, University of Chicago.

Kohlberg, L. (1963) Moral development and identification. In H. Stevenson (ed.) *Child Psychology: 62nd Yearbook of the National Society for the Study of Education*. Chicago: University of Chicago Press.

Kohlberg, L. (1964) Development of moral character and moral ideology. In M. L. Hoffman and L. W. Hoffman (eds) *Review of Child Development Research, I*. New York: Russell Sage Foundation.

Kohlberg, L. (1968) The child as moral philosopher. *Psychology Today* (September), pp. 25–30.

Kohlberg, L. (1969) Stage and sequence: the cognitive-developmental approach to socialization. In D. A. Goslin (ed.) *Handbook of Socialization Theory and Research*. Chicago: Rand McNally.

Kohlberg, L. (1970) Education for justice. In N. F. Sizer and T. R. Sizer (eds) *Moral Education: Five Lectures*. Cambridge, Mass.: Harvard University Press.

Kohlberg, L. (1971) From is to ought: how to commit the naturalistic fallacy and get away with it in the study of moral development. In T. Mischel (ed.) *Cognitive Development and Epistemology*. New York: Academic Press.

Kohlberg, L. (1973) Continuities in childhood and adult moral development revisited. In P. B. Baltes and L. R. Goulet (eds) *Lifespan Developmental Psychology*. New York: Academic Press.

Kohlberg, L. (1976) Moral stages and moralization: the cognitive-developmental approach. In T. Lickona (ed.) *Moral Development and Behaviour*. New York: Holt, Rinehart and Winston.

Kohlberg, L. and Gilligan, C. F. (1971) The adolescent as philosopher; the discovery of the self in a postconventional world. *Daedalus 100*: 1051–6.

Kohlberg, L. and Kramer, R. B. (1969) Continuities and discontinuities in childhood and adult moral development. *Human Development 12*: 93–120.

Kohlberg, L. and Mayer, R. (1972) Development as the aim of education. *Harvard Educational Review 42*: 449–96.

Kohlberg, L., Colby, A., Speicher-Dubin, B. and Power, C. (1977) Assessing moral stages: a manual. Unpublished manuscript, Centre for Moral Education, Harvard.

Kuhn, D., Langer, J., Kohlberg, L. and Haan, N. (1972) The development of formal operations in logical and moral judgement. University of Chicago manuscript.

Kurtines, W. and Greif, E. B. (1974) The development of moral thought. Review and evaluation of Kohlberg's approach. *Psychological Bulletin 81*: 453–70.

Loevinger, J. (1976) *Ego Development*. San Francisco: Jossey-Bass.

Lorimer, R. (1971) Change in the development of moral judgement in adolescence; the effect of structural exposition v. film discussion. *Canadian Journal of Behavioural Science 3*: 1–10.

McDougall, W. (1908) *Social Psychology*. London: Methuen.

Mackinnon, D. W. (1938) Violation of prohibitions. In H. Murray *Explorations in Personality*. Oxford: Oxford University Press.

McNamee, S. (1977) Moral behaviour, moral development and motivation. *Journal of Moral Education 7*: 27–32.

Milgram, S. (1963) Behavioural study of obedience. *Journal of Abnormal and Social Psychology* 67: 371–8.

Milgram, S. (1965) Some conditions of obedience and disobedience to authority. *Human Relations* 18: 57–76.

Milgram, S. (1967) The compulsion to do evil. *Patterns of Prejudice* 1: 3–7.

Mischel, W. and Mischel, H. N. (1976) A cognitive social-learning approach to morality and self-regulation. In T. Lickona (ed.) *Moral Development and Behaviour*. New York: Holt, Rinehart and Winston.

Neill, A. S. (1961) *Summerhill: A Radical Approach to Education*. London: Gollancz.

Peck, R. F. and Havighurst, R. (1960) *The Psychology of Character Development*. New York: Wiley.

Peters, R. S. (1963) Reason and habit: the paradox of moral education. In W. R. Niblett (ed.) *Moral Education in a Changing Society*. London: Faber and Faber.

Peters, R. S. (1971) Moral development: a plea for pluralism. In T. Mischel (ed.) *Cognitive Development and Epistemology*. New York: Academic Press.

Peters, R. S. (1974) Moral development and moral learning. *The Monist* 58.

Piaget, J. (1932) *The Moral Judgement of the Child*. London: Routledge and Kegan Paul.

Pinard, A. and Laurendeau, M. (1969) 'Stage' in Piaget's cognitive-developmental theory. In D. Elkind and J. H. Flavell (eds) *Studies in Cognitive Development*. Oxford: Oxford University Press.

Podd, M. (1972) Ego-identity status and morality. *Developmental Psychology* 6: 497–507.

Puka, W. (1976) Moral education and its cure. In J. R. Meyer (ed.) *Reflections on Values Education*. Ontario: Wilfred Laurier University Press.

Rawls, J. (1971) *A Theory of Justice*. Oxford: Oxford University Press.

Rest, J. R., Turiel, E. and Kohlberg, L. (1969) Level of moral development as a determinant of preference and comprehension of moral judgements made by others. *Journal of Personality* 37: 225–52.

Rest, J. R. (1973) Patterns of preference and comprehension in moral judgement. *Journal of Personality* 41: 86–109.

Rosenhan, D. L. (1969) Some origins of concern for others. In P. Mussen, J. Langer and M. Covington (eds) *Trends and Issues in Developmental Psychology*. New York: Holt, Rinehart and Winston.

Rosenhan, D. L. (1972) Learning theory and pro-social behaviour. *Journal of Social Issues* 28: 151–63.

Rousseau, J. J. (1762) *Emile*. (Everyman edition, 1974, London: Dent.)

Schwartz, S. (1968) Words, deeds and the perception of consequences and responsibility in action situations. *Journal of Personality and Social Psychology* 10: 232–42.

Sears, R. R., Rau, L. and Alpert, R. (1965) *Identification and Child Rearing*. Stanford: Stanford University Press.

Selman, R. L. (1976) Social-cognitive understanding: a guide to educational and clinical practice. In T. Lickona (ed.) *Moral Development and Behaviour*. New York: Holt, Rinehart and Winston.

Skinner, B. F. (1971) *Beyond Freedom and Dignity*. Harmondsworth: Penguin Books.

Solomon, R. L. (1960) Preliminary report on temptation and guilt in young dogs. In O. H. Mowrer (ed.) *Learning Theory and the Symbolic Processes*. New York: Wiley.

Solomon, R. L., Turner, L. H. and Lessac, M. S. (1968) Some effects of delay of punishment on resistance to temptation in dogs. *Journal of Personality and Social Psychology 8*: 233–8.

Sugarman, B. (1973) *The School and Moral Development*, London: Croom Helm.

Sullivan, E. V. (1977) A study of Kohlberg's structural theory of moral development: a critique of liberal social science ideology. *Human Development 20*: 352–76.

Swainson, B. M. (1949) The development of moral ideas in children and adolescents. Unpublished Ph.D. thesis, University of Oxford (cited by Kay, 1968).

Thornton, D. (1977) Criminality and moral reasoning. Paper presented to the International Conference on Moral Development and Moral Education, Leicester, August, 1977.

Trainer, F. E. (1977) A critical analysis of Kohlberg's contributions to the study of moral thought. *Journal of Theory of Social Behaviour 7*: 41–63.

Turiel, E. (1966) An experimental test of the sequentiality of developmental stages in the child's moral judgements. *Journal of Personality and Social Psychology 3*: 611–18.

Turiel, E. (1969) Developmental processes in the child's moral thinking. In P. Mussen, J. Langer and M. Covington (eds) *Trends and Issues in Developmental Psychology*. New York: Holt, Rinehart and Winston.

Walster, E. and Piliavin, J. A. (1972) Equity and the innocent bystander. *Journal of Social Issues 28*: 165–89.

Weinreich, H. E. (1970) A replication and evaluation of a study by Lawrence Kohlberg of the development of moral judgement in the adolescent. Unpublished M.Phil. thesis, University of Sussex.

Weinreich, H. E. (1974) The structure of moral reason. *Journal of Youth and Adolescence 3*: 135–45.

Weinreich, H. E. (1977) Some consequences of replicating Kohlberg's original moral development study on a British sample. *Journal of Moral Education 7*: 32–9.

Weinreich-Haste, H. E. (1977) Some critical questions for Kohlberg. Paper presented to the International Conference on Moral Development and Moral Education, Leicester, August 1977.

Wispé, L. G. (1972) Positive forms of social behaviour; an overview. *Journal of Social Issues 28*: 1–19.

Wright, D. S. (1971) *The Psychology of Moral Behaviour*. Harmondsworth: Penguin.

Wright, D. S. (1976) Some thoughts on moral education. *Journal of Moral Education 6*: 3–6.

Zimbardo, P. G. (1974) On the ethics of intervention in human psychological research: with special reference to the Stanford prison experiment. *Cognition 2*: 243–56.

4 Sex role learning

Elizabeth Douvan

Discussions of sex role and sex identity suffer more than many other discussions in the psychological literature from confusion and careless use of terms. While it may not entirely eliminate confusion, a careful effort to define terms initially may help to illuminate the topic and at least clarify where real problems and gaps in our knowledge exist.

To begin, then, at least four related terms are used commonly in the literature: gender identity, sex role identity, sex identity and sex role. While there is by no means complete consensus about usage, the following definitions are taken from the literature and represent major theorists.

Gender identity refers to an early body-related sense of the self as male or female. Kohlberg (1966) and other investigators find that very young children know that they are boys or girls and show sex-typed preferences before they demonstrate any selective attachment to the same-sex parent. The derivation of this sense of gender from body sources in combination with socialization rather than from identification has been argued by theorists (Bardwick, 1971) and supported by the findings of Money and his colleagues in research on sexual anomaly, gender identity differentiation and dimorphism (Money and Ehrhardt, 1972). Kohlberg's critical review of sex role research (1966) adds support by highlighting the lack of evidence for an identification model of sex role learning. Many of the studies he reviews 'show no relationship between the child's sex role identity and the same-sex parent's Masculinity-Femininity score, the parent's expectation for the child on the M-F dimension, or the presence of the same-sex parent in the home' (Pleck, 1973). If the parent is not the sole source of the child's sense of gender, we must clearly look to body cues, peer relations, and relationships with other adults as determinants. However it develops the early sense of gender is something which the child accepts early and attaches in some primitive way to the body image.

Sex role identity is defined as the sense of one's self as masculine or feminine in social stance and behaviour. This concept refers to the style of performing one's social sex role. It is at once broader and vaguer in reference than gender identity, and it is learned later in life. In fact, as I will try to demonstrate later in this essay, it may well be a salient element in normal identity only during a relatively short period beginning in puberty and subsiding sometime in early adulthood. It treats gender as a trait and ranges people on trait scales of masculinity and femininity. In the psychological literature it underlies all of the early work on M-F scales (Terman and Miles, 1936; Tyler, 1968) and forms part of the background of the new research on androgyny as well (Bem, 1976; Spence and Helmreich, 1978). In everyday matters it underlies adolescent concerns about athletic prowess for males and heterosexual popularity for girls. The concern here is to meet the culture's standards of acceptable sex role performance. Predictably it focuses often (although not exclusively) on superficial aspects of appearance, taste, and behaviour. (Interior decorating is a 'feminine' field, engineering is masculine; ruffles are feminine, muscles are masculine; responding to babies and small animals is feminine). Clearly such concepts are closely bound to the culture defining them.

Sex identity is a concept introduced by Gagnon and Simon (1973) to cover those aspects of the self system which concern specifically sexual behaviour. By late adolescence the individual develops a concept of the self as a sexual being with certain characteristic preferences and styles for performing in the sexual realm: sexually active, sexy, homosexual, sexually inhibited, a 'stud', a Don Juan, a nymphomaniac, a lesbian, a sex goddess; all of these terms refer to sexual identities. Since full sexual identity develops later than the age period covered by 'the school years', it will not be discussed extensively in this paper.

Sex role is a concept which alludes to social or cultural prescriptions about appropriate masculine and feminine behaviour. In the psychological literature it most often merges with the concept of sex identity to become 'sex role identity', that is, the individual's way of being, behaving and defining the self in accordance with the culture's sex role prescriptions.

As a sociological construct, sex role presents certain critical problems. Whenever the concept of role is applied to a social category like gender or class or race, it is in a sense misapplied, for while role refers to functions, categories refer to characteristics of a class. As a sociological concept, role refers to norms (i.e. shared expectations) for behaviour attached to a position in a social system. Thus we can describe the expectations governing the position of foreman in a factory, teacher in a classroom, parent or son or daughter in a family, president of the United States, and so forth. Behaviour in these roles can be more or less accurately predicted irrespective of the particular individual characteristics of the persons performing them, and behaviour which violates the norms for the position will occasion moral indignation and sanctions.

We can conceive and codify the norms and expectations attached to certain sex-linked positions like 'nun', 'priest', 'southern belle', 'liberated woman', 'Don Juan', 'hit man'. These are recognizable roles attached to reciprocal interacting roles in specified social organizations. 'Woman' and 'man' or 'male' and 'female', on the other hand, designate gender but give no or very limited clues about the norms and expectations they carry and no information at all about what social organization they fit into as subparts or elements. They cannot since, as we note in the list of more restrictive, specified roles which carry gender meaning (e.g. nun, hit man, priest), two or more roles which are restricted to males can have contradictory requirements: thus priest and Don Juan, priest and hit man. While these are all equally 'male' they are contradictory or mutually exclusive in their norms and specifications for behaviour. 'Male' by itself, then, does not encompass a coherent or meaningful set of prescriptive norms. Nor does female. People learn and adopt roles which are associated with gender. They do not learn or perform sex roles as such. One might make a case for deference as the sole normative prescription associated with social categories (i.e. 'female' may always imply deference to 'male', 'lower class' to 'upper class', 'minority member' to 'majority member'). Even here the expectation will vary depending on the intersection of social categories (a majority female may expect deference from a minority male in a racist society) or of the social category with more closely specified roles (a female teacher has authority over and expects deference from a male student).

It is only in adolescence that gender takes on normative prescriptions and the qualities of a role in a social system. Around puberty the youngster experiences pressure and imperious expectations from parents and other adults, but most critically from members of the peer group, to perform the role of acceptable male or acceptable female. The role is circumscribed by quite specific behavioural parameters. The boy is to be cool, self-contained, emotionally restrained, competitive and athletic, or at least athletic minded. Above all he is to abjure all signs of dependency. The girl is to be interpersonally adept, sensitive, charming, non-competitive, thoughtful of others, self-effacing, helpful, attractive and popular. Straying beyond the bounds of these prescriptions will cause consternation (if not alarm) in parents and other critical adults, rejection from peers and loss of ground in the heterosexual arena which holds critical rewards: self-affirming acceptance by peers, and self esteem.

How are sex roles learned? What do adults and the community of peers communicate to youngsters in critical developmental periods about the meaning of maleness and femaleness, the demands, opportunities and limitations imposed and provided by sex roles? We can distinguish fruitfully between childhood and adolescence in this discussion.

Sex role learning in childhood

Until recently the dominant theory of sex role development centred on the concept of identification, a legacy from Freudian thought. According to this view the little male or female makes a decisive identification with the same-sex parent in order to manage intrapsychic and real conflict stimulated by Oedipal longing for sole possession of the parent of the other sex. Through identification – by becoming psychically the father – the little male is able to realize his unconscious desires on an intrapsychic level. Identification leads to repression in this scheme.

More recently Kohlberg (1966) and Mischel (1970) have suggested alternative models of sex role learning. Mischel offers a social learning theory of sex role identity (see Chapter 3). Kohlberg's review of research brought the identification model under serious question, and he as well as Block (1973) offer a cognitive developmental model as an alternative. According to this view the child's conception of sex roles develops through specific stages comparable to those obtaining in other areas of cognitive development. Where morality is concerned, for example, concepts develop from an initial stage during which ideas are relatively amorphous and confused, to an intermediate phase in which the rules are understood and applied rigidly and defensively, and finally to a stage in which understanding combines with flexibility and appreciation for individual differences. Sex role development may, according to Kohlberg, be conceived in a similar developmental scheme with the final 'mature' stage being the relatively loose and flexible application of sex role conceptions we designate as androgyny.

The cognitive developmental model fits the research data and observations from life. Gender identity – the gender label little children know early and connect to body, body image and a vague sense of destiny – is by no means a refined or technically accurate concept. And it has little to do with sex role concepts. That is, it does not carry accurate differential designations of behaviour expected or possible for a boy or a girl. The little boy at three still may think he will have babies, a little girl may want to become Joe Frazier. Throughout childhood the label remains but gradually takes on more and more refined contents. By six or so the little girl believes that she will be a woman and mother, the little boy that he will be a man and father. Parents have significant effects on this developing concept, but other people and other sources available more broadly in the culture (e.g. the media, textbooks, etc.) undoubtedly also contribute to the development.

Among older children we often observe the tightening, the rigid application of sex role rules that Kohlberg's thesis would lead us to expect. Boys and girls begin to play in groups which are much more exclusive by sex. Boys talk about 'catching girl germs' and avoid contact with all things female even within their families. We know from older studies of sex-linked interests that females show a peaking of feminine interests around the age of fourteen and males peak in sex-linked interests somewhat later (Terman and Miles, 1936). It is as though youngsters defend their sense of sex role adequacy until sometime in adolescence by tightening definitions and narrowing interests. Once sex role identity is formed and legitimated, young males and females relax and loosen restrictive rules in the sex role area as in the sphere of moral behaviour.

Adolescence

Sex is always interesting to children. The anthropologists have disabused us of naive belief in the Freudian notion of a latency period in which children put aside the issue of sex in a decisive act of repression bolstered by other defences. And once questioned, the idea falls victim to common sense and simple observation of behaviours we had not been able to see so long as the culture supported the view that children from five to twelve were sexless. All children seek information about the secret of adulthood, well hidden in earlier generations and now displayed on every news stand. Poor children, rural children and children in pre-literate cultures never had to strain for instruction since the rude conditions of life – crowding and lack of privacy, or closeness to nature – offered plentiful opportunity to learn and observe. But even heavily protected urban middle class children growing up under the sway of Victorian remnants read the Bible and knew the sexual allusions, found the library of a friend's physician father a rich resource, discovered literature and its sexual treasures, observed older peers flirting and courting, even knew from the world of art that certain parts of the body were special from their adornment with fig leaves. The curiosity and imagination of children are without limit and hold enormous power. Think of the range and variety of theories of reproduction created through the ages by lively young minds driven by the spike of sexual curiosity – a marvel now more or less destroyed by sex education.

Yet the idea of the latency period holds a kernel of truth in that sexual interests *are* different after puberty. Freud described the difference as residing in the aim or goal of the drive. Infantile sexuality, he said, is without specific aim, limitless, with no definable end state. Genital sexuality, on the other hand, has a goal, the achievement of which resolves the drive temporarily.

One can also phrase the difference in quantitative terms: the radical increase in circulating levels of hormones at puberty and the development of the sex organs and secondary sexual characteristics have as their psychic counterpart an intensification of sexual interest, an increased sexual tension. Accelerated sex drive has no immediate outlet, and it is this imbalance among other things which motivates the adolescent to learn meaningful, acceptable and effective ways of being male or female. To realize sexual fulfilment – whether direct or sublimated in form – requires learning to be an acceptable woman or man, female or male.

Empirical studies clearly demonstrate the intensified drive at puberty in males. The Kinsey data (1953), as well as studies of other samples (Sanford, 1943; Symonds, 1949), reveal increased sexual behaviour and fantasy. Females do not show equivalent quickening in sexual interests, behaviour, or fantasy. They show rather an increase in themes of self abasement in fantasy productions, which have been interpreted as signs of guilt and the repression of sexual drive (Douvan, 1970).

The difference in expression of sex drive in adolescent males and females – the fact that it is more susceptible to repression and/or sublimation in females – has been tied to differences in the biological statement of sex at puberty (Chilman, 1977; Douvan, 1970; Bardwick, 1971). For the male the drive is relatively clear and explicitly stated in external organs which are known and familiar sources of pleasure. In the female the primary sex organs are internal and hidden and awakening sexuality takes more diffuse and ambiguous forms – skin sensitivity, vaginal lubrication and diffuse pelvic excitation. The male task of erotic resolution consists of detaching cathexis from the nuclear family and transferring erotic interest to an eligible female peer. Learning to express sexual love and winning a desired partner are sometimes hard and painful tasks. But the male at least knows the nature and seat of his drive in a clear and explicit way which is not biologically given to the female. She must first piece out the nature and meaning of her sexual drive. She does this in part through experimentation but also, and probably in somewhat larger part, through intimate interpersonal sharing of feelings, information, meanings with other girls. Among the effects of her more ambiguous sexuality, then, we can list the girl's somewhat later experience with most forms of explicit sexual expression (cf. Kinsey et al., 1953) compared to boys', and her more highly developed intimate friendships (Douvan and Adelson, 1966). Girls are encouraged in interpersonal skills thoughout their early socialization, and at adolescence they are also driven by internal needs to develop and use these skills in friendship for self-exploration and the acquisition of crucial self-knowledge.

Sex role expectations at adolescence

We know from Kagan and Moss's longitudinal studies that certain behaviours are differentially continuous or discontinuous in the development of males and females from pre-school through early adulthood (1962). Females show discontinuity in aggressiveness and relative continuity in dependency. The pattern is reversed in males. More important for the present discussion is their conclusion that the discontinuities stem from the fact that certain characteristics conflict with sex role expectations which the culture imposes most stringently around puberty. It is as though parents and other adults see adolescence as a last chance to ensure that the child effectively identifies with that most primitive reference group and consolidates a sense of his/her appropriate gender. Characteristics that conflict with sex identity are discouraged in overt form and must find more indirect and sublimated expression. Aggressiveness in the girl and dependency/passivity in the boy move from the playground to the academic/intellectual realm. Parents may be tolerant of a little boy's interest in cooking and homemaking and a little girl's interest in competitive sports, but around puberty they begin to press for more clearly sex-appropriate choices and expressions – as though this were a new, more serious game 'for keeps' and any deviation thus more ominous.

Kagan also makes a theoretical point of the sex difference in opportunities for self-testing in adolescence (Kagan, 1966). While the boy is more likely to have additional access to information and feedback about the self which does not depend on the evaluation and response of others, the girl, he suggests, must continue to rely on social response for self-affirmation. So, for example, the boy can know how good he is at hitting baskets with a ball even when he practises alone; the girl, on the other hand, can know how effective she is in social skill, in winning the affection and regard of others, only from the reaction of those others. Her sense of adequacy depends on an audience and continues to encourage her in her childhood stance of other-directedness and reliance on others.

It is not only parents' expectations that sensitize adolescents to sex roles. Peers and the high school peer culture most critically impose sex role norms, as I shall describe shortly. But adults other than parents also communicate these expectations. In a recent study of high schools, my colleagues and I found evidence of sex role norms operating both subtly and overtly in the behaviour and expectations of teachers and other school personnel and in the official reward system of high schools.

Students are aware of these effects. For example, girl students know and complain of the fact that their athletic programme does not have resources or backing from teachers and the school system comparable to the male interscholastic programme. They know that 'teachers don't think girls' sports are important. The know that we're not going to be professional athletes so they just don't care.' We also heard many similar complaints from the women students (as well as students in non-academic vocational programmes in the schools) about the counselling services offered by these schools. ('If you're not a college-bound male, they figure you don't need counselling. They think girls are just going to marry anyway and vocational students will go to the factory. They're only there to help boys decide which college to go to or what programme to take in the university.')

Since they also act as models, the behaviour of teachers in itself communicates sex role expectations. Male teachers in the schools we studied were more extensively involved with students than are female teachers. While the two groups spent equal in-class time with students (according to their reports in response to questionnaires), male teachers spent more time supervising extracurricular activities – coaching and sponsoring after-school interest clubs and groups. Or, looked in a somewhat different way, women teachers spent equal time with male and female students, while male teachers spent much more time with male students than with female students. Female teachers spent more time in social interaction among themselves and at home with their families. Again, the message being put across to the students seemed to be that males warrant more resources because of the importance of school for their vocational futures.

We observed many instances of subtle communication to students of the message that males work and females serve. I will add just one finding from our studies which seems to indicate that boys have access to somewhat more than their share of academic rewards through their participation in interscholastic athletics. We found that males on varsity teams had grade point averages higher than one would predict on the basis of ability tests alone. The need to keep their grades up to ensure eligibility for team sports may contribute to this finding (and if so, one would like to develop comparable incentives for non-athletes) but it seems possible to us that the boy's participation and contribution to school spirit may also create a halo of good citizenship which subtly affects teachers' evaluations in ambiguous, borderline areas of judgement.

Coleman's study of the high school culture demonstrates that the peer society rewards and punishes adolescents according to their adherance to sex role expectations (Coleman, 1961). Success in the adolescent social world depended on meeting sex-linked criteria. Such success required athletic performance for boys and social leadership for girls, and the youngsters themselves recognized and valued these activities above academic achievement. As they moved through the high school years, however, boys came to value academic achievement more (though never more than athletic prowess) but girls valued academic achievement even less in the final year of high school than they had earlier. This suggests that sex role bears more heavily on girls and that it presents girls with a conflict between sex role expectations and cultural criteria of success.

Formation of heterosexual friendships and the institution of dating contribute to developing sex role concepts in adolescence. In the United States girls begin to date in middle adolescence, around 14, boys begin about a year later. The dating arena has been described by Mead (1949) and others as a competitive achievement sphere. And, at least in initial phases, heterosexual interaction does bear the stamp of an instrumental activity, the important goal of which is to demonstrate to peers that one is desirable. Data from interviews with girls reveal that through the early stages of dating girls' relationships with boyfriends are defensive and instrumental and share little of the mutuality and intimacy which girls' like-sexed friendships have developed by this time. During middle adolescence the girl's interaction with 'dates' has the quality of a role relationship: as long as she has a 'date' to go out with, be seen with, the particular individual who fills the role is relatively unimportant. Only in later adolescence do heterosexual friendships develop into interactive interpersonal relationships (Douvan and Adelson, 1966).

None the less, dating contributes to adolescents' concepts of acceptable sex role behaviour and provides opportunities for youngsters to practise ways of being male or female in heterosexual social exchange. For girls, at least, success and appropriate pacing in dating relate to overall measures of ego-development and self-esteem (Douvan and Adelson, op. cit.).

Sex role and self-concept

Studies of adolescent self-concept indicate that sex role identity and adequacy are central to self-definition at this period and that sex-linked interests and goals come to dominate adolescents' behaviour in the present and plans for the future.

Coleman's finding that peer values emphasize athletic prowess for boys and social leadership and popularity for girls indicates pre-occupation with sex role, the need to establish public recognition of one's male or female adequacy.

The world of work focuses and concretizes a great deal of boys' adolescent preoccupation. Boys engage in active sorting and selecting of future job prospects, testing possible jobs against the reality of individual talent and taste. Their vocational aspirations are highly differentiated by middle adolescence and boys have by this period also integrated instrumental educational plans to their ideas about a future work. Girls, on the other hand, hold less articulated and differentiated vocational aspirations, more clearly dominated by sex role stereotypes, and they have less developed ideas about the educational requirements for the jobs they choose.

The level of job aspiration girls choose is clearly coordinated to their family plans, while boys show no such contingency in their choice of jobs. In our recent study of high school youth, we found that those girls who thought they would marry relatively early and have large families conditioned their occupational plans accordingly. Those girls who held plans for high status occupations tended to post-pone marriage and motherhood in their concepts of the future. Male adolescents – in keeping with the culture's sex assignment of tasks, did not show this coordination between job and family plans (Locksley and Douvan, 1978).

Sex role conflict

Identification theorists have noted the fact that all babies initially focus attachment and affection on a female figure and have concluded that the male thus carries a residual feminine identification which complicates and potentially jeopardizes his ultimate masculine resolution. The apparently greater incidence of male homosexuality (compared to lesbianism) is adduced as evidence of the more complex and fragile masculine identification.

One can usefully cast this issue more generally by taking account of any discontinuity as a source of complication in sex role learning. In this frame one can see complications in sex role socialization for both males and females. All babies experience the first attachment to the mother, and all babies are feminine in the stereotypic sense: that is, passive and dependent on others for gratification and for a sense of self. At or around two-and-a-half the male child must give up infancy and make himself a little boy. This represents a discontinuity and a crisis for the male child which is not posed for the female who can continue in a passive dependent stance.

At or around adolescence, however, the girl encounters her critical discontinuity. Socialized through childhood in a double system – in which she is allowed dependency but is also encouraged and supported through school to be independent, individualistic, competitive and achieving, she now finds at adolescence that she must abandon or disguise these individual competitive traits if she is to be acceptably feminine. Adults and especially her peer group expect her to shift from direct achievement to vicarious achievement and take as her major goals becoming a wife and mother. She learns that to be popular – and especially popular in the heterosexual game – she must draw in her assertive, competitive tendencies and again define herself by her relationship to others rather than her own achievements and independent traits. Boys, she finds, do not like aggressive girls and certainly do not want to be bested in competition by girls. Both the future and the present suddenly restrict her expression to those aspects of her behaviour which emphasize winning and holding the affection of others. She is asked to give up established ways of being and behaving, ways practised throughout the primary school years. Abandoning established patterns represents her critical discontinuity, just as giving up the ways of infancy represents discontinuity for the two-and-a-half-year-old boy.

Each of these crises takes a toll in adjustment, stress, and satisfaction. Throughout childhood, the male presents more behaviour problems and developmental disturbances than the female. But sometime around puberty girls begin to show signs of conflict and maladaptation which can be seen as the outcome of the discontinuity in expectations they encounter, the sudden imposition of sex role expectations which narrow and restrict girls' options.

In our study of Detroit high schools (Locksley and Douvan, 1978) we found evidence that actual achievement in school reduces stress among boys but not among girls, and that meeting adult expectations reduces stress among girls but not among boys. We found further that the salience of sex-linked goals for girls relates negatively to achievement goals, and that achievement is generally conflictful for girls.

We theorized that achievement during high school can be usefully segregated into two quite different aspects: one consists of meeting adult expectations for the student role, the other consists of actual academic performance according to relatively objective standards. We speculated that in many American high schools, objective performance (i.e. obtaining high grades) would facilitate boys' overall adaptation because it represents sex role congruent achievement and is coinage in the competitive arena of peer society. Meeting adult expectations, however, should be conflictful for boys because of its implications for autonomy. For girls, on the other hand, objective achievement conflicts with sex role norms while meeting adult expectations does not.

We measured objective performance by grades and meeting adult expectations by two series of questions which asked students both how much parents and teacher expected certain behaviours (e.g. 'that you will speak up in class', 'that you will complete all your assignments', 'that you will do well in school') and how well they felt they were able to meet these expectations. We then related these measures to measures of stress, and found evidence supporting our predictions. That is, boys' objective performance showed a clear relationship to measures of stress (the higher the grades, the lower the stress) but meeting adult expectations for the student role did not relate to stress reduction. For girls the relationships were reversed; that is, objective performance was not related to adjustment, but meeting adult expectations for student role performance did relate to lower stress.

We found, in addition, other evidence of girls' conflict over objective achievement and future job plans. For one thing we found that for every level of job aspiration, and for every level of educational aspiration, girls showed a higher actual grade point average than boys. For example, girls, who have no plans for education beyond high school have a grade point average higher than the average of boys who plan to go to college. Girls who anticipate working in the lowest status occupations earn a higher grade point average than boys who anticipate working in medium status occupations. It is as though for girls present objective success in school does not feed into future planning (Locksley and Douvan, 1978).

I have alluded earlier to the contingency that marks girls' educational and occupational plans, the fact that marriage and family plans condition the girls' occupational choices in a way which is not true for boys. Finally, we find that girls with high grade point averages show greater depression and more psychosomatic symptoms than do boys who earn high averages or girls who have medium averages (Locksley and Douvan, 1978). In all, the evidence strongly supports the view that at adolescence girls confront serious conflict between sex role norms and the culture's values of individual achievement and success.

Summary

The period from 6 to 18 encompasses most sex role learning. One might even assert with some legitimacy that it includes the only stages in life when the sex role is salient for most people. A perusal of the new literature on sex roles/sex identity reveals that only a minority of any sampled population of adults falls outside the 'androgynous' category. Initially this could be attributed to the education level of respondents – early studies (Spence, 1978; Bem, 1976) used college students who had experienced the androgynizing effects of higher education (Sanford, 1943). But we now have data from adult samples and non-college samples (Tucker, 1978; Colten, 1977) which show the same pattern. Only about a quarter of the group score highly 'feminine' or highly 'masculine'. Most people fall in the mixed categories: androgynous or undifferentiated.

This makes very good sense. Most adults have settled on self-concepts which include sex role but are by no means dominated by it. Unless their lives suffer major disruption which puts them again into the heterosexual market, the issue rests unattended in the nexus of assumed self attitudes. Most women know that the occupational world segregates and discriminates against them, and resurgent feminism has reminded us all of this and other sex-linked realities. But feminism presses for reducing the relevance of gender rather than increasing it.

Sex role identity is critical during adolescence when the culture, the parents and the peer group all bear in on the youngster the need to align with the appropriate gender group. The peer society in particular communicates quite specific standards of appropriate masculine and feminine behaviour, and metes out rewards and punishments for conforming to or violating these norms. Sex role norms for the young female conflict with individualist, competitive, achievement values in the culture and create for her certain conflicts about achievement and future planning.

References

Bardwick, J. (1971) *The Psychology of Women.* New York: Harper and Row.
Bem, S. (1976) Probing the promise of androgyny. In A. G. Kaplan and J. Bean (eds) *Beyond Sex-Role Stereotypes: Readings toward a Psychology of Androgyny.* Boston: Little, Brown.
Block, J. (1973) Conceptions of sex role: some cross-cultural and longitudinal perspectives. *American Psychologist 28*: 512–26.
Chilman, C. (1977) *Social and Psychological Aspects of Adolescent Sexuality.* Milwaukee: University of Wisconsin School of Social Welfare.
Coleman, J. S. (1961) *The Adolescent Society.* New York: The Free Press.
Colten, M. E. (1977) A descriptive and comparative analysis of self perceptions of heroin-addicted women. Unpublished manuscript, Ann Arbor: Institute for Social Research.
Douvan, E. and Adelson, J. (1966) *The Adolescent Experience.* New York: Wiley.
Douvan, E. (1970) New sources of conflict in adolescence. In J. Bardwick, E. Douvan, M. Horner and D. Gutman (eds) *Feminine Personality and Conflict.* Belmont, Calif.: Brooks Cole.
Dreyer, P. (1977) Research trends in adolescent sex role identity. Paper presented at the American Psychological Association, San Francisco, Calif., 1977.
Gagnon, J. and Simon, W. (1973) *The Sexual Scene,* Chicago: Aldine.
Kagan, J. (1966) Acquisition and significance of sex typing and sex role identity. In M. L. Hoffman and L. W. Hoffman (eds) *Review of Child Development Research 1.* New York: Russell Sage.
Kagan, J. and Moss, H. (1962) *Birth to Maturity.* New York: Wiley.
Kinsey, A. C., Pomeroy, W., Martin, C. and Gebhard, W. (1953) *Sexual Behavior in the Human Female.* Philadelphia: W. B. Saunders.
Kohlberg, L. A. (1966) Cognitive-developmental analysis of children's sex role concepts and attitudes. In E. Maccoby (ed.), *The Development of Sex Differences.* Stanford: Stanford University Press.
Locksley, A. and Douvan, E. (1978) Problem behavior in adolescents. In E. Gomberg and V. Frank (eds) *Sex Differences in Disturbed Behavior.* New York: Bruner Mazel.
Mead, M. (1949) *Male and Female.* New York: Morrow.
Mischel, W. (1970) Sex-typing and socialization. In P. Mussen (ed.) *Carmichael's Manual of Child Psychology* (third edition). New York: Wiley.

Money, J. and Ehrhardt, A. A. (1972) *Man and Woman, Boy and Girl*. Baltimore: The Johns Hopkins University Press.

Pleck, J. (1973) New concepts of sex role identity. Paper presented at the Society for the Scientific Study of Sex, New York, November 1973.

Sanford, N. (1943) Personality development and scholarship. *Monograph of the Society for Research in Child Development* No. 1.

Spence, J. and Helmreich, W. (1978) *Masculinity and Femininity*. Austin, Texas: University of Texas Press.

Symonds, P. M. (1949) *Adolescent Phantasy*. New York: Columbia University Press.

Terman, L. and Miles, C. (1936) *Sex and Personality*. New York: McGraw-Hill.

Tucker, M. (1978) Support systems among addicted and non-addicted women. Paper presented at the National Drug Abuse Conference, Seattle, April 1978.

Tyler, L. (1968) Individual differences: sex differences. In D. Sills (ed.) *International Encyclopedia of the Social Sciences*. New York: Macmillan.

5 The role of the peer group

Phillida Salmon

The concept of the peer group

In the literature about children's social-psychological development the peer group has long been seen as a topic of importance. It constitutes a chapter heading in many texts, it features as the focus of investigation in a large number of empirical studies and, as a concept, it plays a large part in general accounts of psychological development during childhood and adolescence. Broadly, the term is used to refer to all social relationships (other than kinship ones) that exist between young people; more specifically, it may denote either group or dyadic relationships. It can fairly be said, therefore, that the area defined by the peer group is a large one and that there is a general consensus among psychologists that it has considerable developmental importance.

Beyond this general consensus, certain other concerns and assumptions seem to be shared by most of the psychologists whose interests have centred on this topic. In particular, certain questions have characteristically been asked in studies of children's peer group relationships, rather than other kinds of questions which might have been put. Similarly, certain methodological biases are evident in the research concerned with this topic. It is also apparent that a number of general assumptions about the nature of children's peer groups have, without necessarily being made explicit, constituted the conceptual basis for the majority of studies that have been carried out. In this chapter an attempt will be made to elucidate these common themes by an overview of the work so far published and to evaluate them critically. Following this some attention will be given to the different social settings in which young people's peer groups are likely to exist. Finally, the question will be taken up of the function, both concurrently and developmentally, that peer group relationships may serve for children and adolescents.

Underlying the trends in the literature, perhaps, are certain long-held assumptions about the nature of children's peer group relationships. What are these assumptions and how far are they justified? Implicit in the bias of investigations to date, with respect to age and gender, is the assumption that the peer group is vastly more significant at adolescence than at other ages, and for boys as against girls. Under-lying this assumption is a view of psychological development as entail-ing a special dependence on age and sex peers at the adolescent period, and of such dependence being particularly the case for males because of the nature of their social role. Yet in so far as evidence exists as to this imbalance, it cannot be said to justify such an assumption. As Hartup (1970), reviewing the whole body of literature, puts it, 'There is little evidence to suggest that group norms are either more or less pervasive in informal peer groups in adolescence than during middle childhood'. When it comes to gender differences, no investigation has actually shown that peers are less significant for girls than for boys, though several studies suggest that the kind of psychological significance may be different. Perhaps the persistence of both these beliefs, however unsubstantiated, is a function of the myths which our society characteristically projects upon adolescents, and particularly upon adolescent boys. In an essay entitled 'Adoles-cents and groups, subcultures and countercultures', Paul Upson (1975) describes this phenomenon in these terms: 'It is the misfortune of adolescents that, in the modern world, it is their destiny always to be seen as the barbarian hordes who threaten civilization itself.'

In that the prevailing view of male adolescent groups is of a pre-dominantly anti-adult society, this seems to be the place to question another typical assumption made by most investigators in the sphere of peer group relationships – the polarization of peer group and adult group norms. This assumption has been effectively challenged by Coleman (1978) who, drawing on a number of American and British studies, shows that the picture of a simple opposition of adult (especially parent) and peer values and pressures is quite untenable. As Coleman remarks, 'The simplistic notion of a serious divergence of attitude and belief between the generations has clouded the picture'. Coleman himself suggests that congruence between adult and peer norms is much greater than is generally assumed: where non-congruence prevails this may be related to the fact that different spheres of experience are involved (Brittain's (1968) situational hypothesis), or that for some reason the individual lacks access to adult views. To this analysis might be added the argument that universality of adult-peer polarization should not be assumed even when it is shown to exist in particular situations, since different cultural contexts may themselves be responsible for inter-generational conflict or harmony, as Bronfenbrenner (1970) has shown in relation to American and Russian contexts. Finally, it may well be that where opposition is found between the two kinds of norm this is an artifact of the kind of measure used.

Still more fundamentally, the very definition of the peer group as implied by much of the literature seems to require a critical re-evaluation. The term is used very loosely to cover relationships with individual age-mates, membership of a small interacting group, activity within an aggregate of relative strangers, attitudes towards the individual's nominal age category, or membership of a vaguely defined youth culture. The implications of continuity, contact and familiarity contained in the word group are obviously less easily justified in some of these usages than in others, and in some, they seem wholly unjustified. The word peer also seems more appropriate to some definitions than to others. Peer means like, or equal, and hence implies some reference to phenomenological reality. All too often, however, no such reference is made. The individual's own sense of similarity or difference is probably frequently violated in the investigator's definition of his peer group, just as his likes and dislikes, feelings of envy, fear, admiration or indifference are characteristically ignored. The failure to attend to these features seems to be the consequence of an approach which defines children's peers essentially from the outside rather than the inside. Hence, age and gender – aspects of children which are salient for the investigator, and perhaps for adults generally – are used to define 'peerness' despite the fact that these characteristics may not be the most significant ones for children – particularly in contexts which have already segregated children in terms of these very categories.

Another assumption that seems implicit in this sphere is that children's peer groups can be considered without reference to their ecology. Yet relationships with other children do not occur in a social vacuum; and a consideration of the institutional and attitudinal settings in which children live seems crucial to an understanding of children's groups.

Let us examine how far these assumptions about children's peer group relationships have in fact influenced the work that has been done in this sphere. With regard to assumptions about age and gender, in relation to the peer group, the influence seems clear. Across the age range between infancy and adulthood certain periods feature much more often than others. Few investigators have studied peer group relationships among children younger than nursery school age. That age group, however, has been the focus for a small number of studies, which have typically examined their subjects within some kind of institutional context, such as that of a nursery school. The Charlesworth and Hartup (1967) study, which looked at levels of positive reinforcement in the interactions of children aged 2 to 5 years in nursery groups, is fairly representative of such investigations. With older children the early school years have received relatively little attention; but middle childhood has been studied more extensively. Of studies which have focused on the peer group at this age probably the most extensive and influential have been the semi-naturalistic investigations of the Sherifs (1964). This work was, of course, concerned with the emergence and functioning of normative peer groups in informal settings, and with the effects of reorganizing interventions by adults. However, if all the studies of the peer group among children younger than adolescent were to be added together, the number would still fall far short of the vast pile of studies of the peer group in adolescence. Such studies range from a focus on informal groups, like that of Patrick (1973), to a focus on groups formed in school settings, like that of Willems (1967); from an interest in the operation of norms, such as the work of Delamont (1976), to a concern with the characteristics of acceptance and rejection, as in the studies of Douvan and Adelson (1966).

When it comes to gender, a similar imbalance exists as that for age. Although the number of boys and girls studied in investigations of the peer group are probably about equal for children younger than about 8, after this age boys are increasingly over-represented.

Distinctive trends are also evident when one looks at the methods

that have been used to study the peer group. Here, the typical investigation of peer group relationships independently of their setting
reveals the assumption that ecological considerations are unimportant. Until recently, the predominant bias has been towards the use
of pencil-and-paper tests of one sort or another. The early favourite
was sociometry in some form, as, for example, in the influential study
of Northway (1943). Sociometric techniques have continued to be
used ever since, and have constituted the basis of assessment in a
substantial proportion of recent studies; the quite large-scale investigation of Horowitz (1967) into friendship patterns among
American school-age children is representative of such studies. In the
last twenty years or so, however, other pencil-and-paper tests have
been introduced into this area by a number of investigators. Of these,
both standard questionnaires, such as the one devised by J. S. Coleman
(1961), and projective techniques, like the sentence completion task
used by J. C. Coleman (1974), have been chosen to assess aspects
of peer group relationships and adjustment, as have some forms of
repertory grid technique (Nash, 1973). Some other studies have relied
on more open-ended forms of assessing instrument; Douvan and
Adelson (1966), for instance, used a semi-structured interview with
the adolescents in their study. Experimental approaches to the assessment of children's peer groups have been much less evident than
pencil-and-paper ones. The often-quoted pioneer study of Lewin,
Lippitt and White (1938) into the effects of leadership climates on
children's groups, did of course show that such an approach was
feasible. But this lead has not really been followed up except where
conformity to peer group norms is concerned. On this topic, manipula-
tive experimental situations form the typical paradigm of investigation. Currently, if any trend is emerging in the methods adopted to
study the peer group it seems to be towards the use of naturalistic
methods. Again, the use of such methods has quite a long history,
dating back to the work of the Sherifs (1964) on children's groups
in informal settings. Until recently, however, naturalistic approaches
to assessment have been relatively neglected. That their potential
fruitfulness may be being currently recognized is suggested by such
studies as that of Patrick (1973) into delinquent gangs, and by the
influential and proliferating investigations of children's classroom
groups undertaken by such workers as Delamont, Walker and Adelman (Stubbs and Delamont, 1976). Among such studies, some form
of participant observation tends to be preferred over the traditional

kind of detached observation. Such trends seem to promise a much-needed attention to the social settings in which peer groups function.

In studies of the peer group during childhood and adolescence it is also obvious that certain kinds of question have tended to predominate. These can perhaps be subsumed under four headings: group composition, group structure, acceptance and influence. Here again, the relative neglect of ecological factors, as well as an attention to product rather than process, seems to underlie the choice of topic.

Questions about the *composition* of the peer group have been central to both older and more recent studies. Usually the concern has been with the relative homogeneity of children's groups in terms, for example, of age, sex, ethnicity, socio-economic background, or ability. An early study which serves to exemplify this approach is that of Parten (1933), involving children aged from 2 to 5 years. More recently, Dunphy's (1972) investigation of adolescent school cliques in Australia, was concerned with the degree of similarity among clique members in socio-economic class, grade level, interests and values. Size of group has been another focus; Dunphy's work incorporated a concern with peer group size in relation to developmental level, while the Douvan and Adelson study (1966) examined differences in friendship group size in relation to gender.

In some other studies, group size has been related to questions of the second type – the *structure* of the peer group. For example, size of group was found to be negatively related to group cohesiveness in Hare's (1952) investigation of boy scout groups of 5 and 12 members. A different aspect of group cohesiveness has been its relationship with age. This is a topic with which several early studies were concerned, as, for example, that of Smith (1960) which showed increasing cohesiveness and stability with age from pre-school to middle childhood peer groups. Group structure also, of course, involves questions about group role; and this is one of the aspects looked at in the studies of the Sherifs (1964). Perhaps because this feature does not readily lend itself to study by formal, quantifying methodologies, the other type of work, besides that of the Sherifs, which has focused on group roles has been the naturalistic study of boys' gangs; the work of Thrasher (1927) examining leaders, lieutenants and followers in semi-delinquent boys' groups, serves as an example.

Again, this sort of question can be seen to be linked to the next question – that of *acceptance*; and some investigators have emphasized the relationship between personal popularity and distinctive group role. In the main, however, work on the topic of group acceptance has concerned itself with determining the correlates of popularity and rejection. Among the many aspects of individual difference that have been looked at are birth order (Lewis and Rosenblum, 1975), child-rearing antecedents (Peck, 1958), rate of pubertal maturity (Jones, 1958), and a huge range of personality characteristics, from cheerfulness and sociability (Wheeler, 1961) to interest in sport (Horowitz, 1967) and attitude similarity (Cavior and Dokecki, 1973).

It would be possible, by drawing on the work of such investigators as, for example, Harvey and Rutherford (1960) to show a link between questions of group acceptance and the last kind of question – group *influence*. Again, however, this last question has typically been studied without reference to peer group acceptance. Nevertheless, many investigators have concerned themselves with other correlates of yielding to peer group influence. One example of this line of work is the study of Costanzo (1970), which assessed the relation between conformity and the degree of self-blame. Within this area, the majority of recent studies have been concerned with the differences between various contexts in which conformity can occur; and here, an attention to ecology is evident. This concern can be seen in the comparison of conforming to parent or peer group wishes according to the character of the dilemma; the view of parents and peers as competent guides in different areas is one which Brittain (1968) has argued from his research into differential conforming. The same concern can be seen in the distinction drawn by Bronfenbrenner (1970) between the cultural contexts available in American and Soviet society and the degree of polarization of adult and peer group norms. It is this distinction which underpins Bronfenbrenner's studies of cross-pressure conforming among American and Russian children.

It seems, therefore, that much of the work concerned with peer group relationships in childhood and adolescence has been based on certain widely held but possibly unfounded views as to the nature of such relationships. These views seem to have influenced the kinds of individual selected for study, the sorts of methods adopted, and the questions that have been put at issue in investigations. It seems also, however, that the kinds of assumptions involved are increasingly being questioned and that trends towards a different direction of investigation are beginning to emerge. Since one of the most important aspects concerns ecological considerations, it is to this sphere that we will now turn.

The ecology of peer relationships

A consideration of the human ecology in which relationships are formed between the young must involve taking into account certain major societal differences. One of the most important of these is probably the degree to which young members of the society are segregated from older ones. As Ariés, the social historian, has pointed out, such segregation is of relatively recent origin in our own society; in mediaeval Europe children and adolescents were closely integrated into every aspect of adult life, and it was only with the advent of industrialization and the institution of schooling which it brought, that the young came to be separated so visibly and so extensively from the older members of their society (Ariés, 1962). This separation is, of course, far less evident in the traditions and practices of many societies whose members now live in this country as minority ethnic groups; and this is likely to affect the way in which peer group relationships are viewed and treated within such groups. Although this area appears to have received very little attention, one illustrative study may be cited which indicates the significance of such differences for a small but enduring subgroup within our own society. In a small-scale study of a gypsy community in Surrey, Sturt (1976) found some wide differences in the composition of social reference groups for gypsy children attending primary school and control children at the same school. Whereas the reference group for the non-gypsy children was composed of same age friends, that for the gypsy children consisted of as many adults as children. It seems that living in a community where contact with adults and their concerns is part of everyday experience makes for friendship and interaction patterns which do not show the usual homogeneity with respect to age. At the opposite extreme, the grim and harsh social context experienced by the small group of children described by Freud and Dann (1951) produced so exclusive a loyalty to each other as to prevent the formation of any other affectional bonds at all, even after many years following their concentration camp incarceration.

A different dimension of comparison between the social contexts in which peer group relationships exist is the extent to which the society as a whole concerns itself with such relationships. There seems to be a general agreement among several writers who have considered this question that the US represents the extreme position on this dimension. Miller and Swanson (1958), for instance, put the case that American society has moved from an entrepreneurial mode where qualities of initiative and individualism were valued, to a bureaucratic mode where cooperativeness and affiliation are prized above all else. From a different point of view, Riesman (1950) argues that present-day American society requires a highly – in his view, excessively – outer-directed adjustment. A third writer, who supports his argument by reference to his own research survey, is Henry (1963). Henry suggests that the extreme mobility in present-day America has given rise to an acute concern with interpersonal relationships – a concern which is evident in the responses of the children and adolescents he studied. Henry's own words are worth quoting on this question:

> In America, the absence of predetermined personal communities plus great mobility brings it about that in one of the great populations of the world, people have become scarce commodities and compete with one another for one another as industry competes for natural resources, for manufactured objects and for consumers. The fact that everyone can be chosen or rejected by others, that he never knows why he is rejected, if he is, and the fact that those he numbered in his personal community one day may not be there the next, makes for enormous uncertainty in interpersonal relations; it makes for great sensitivity to looks, stares, smiles and criticism, and originates the endless inner questioning, 'Am I liked?'.

The significance of this kind of concern must have many ramifications. The establishing and maintaining of peer group relationships are likely to be highly important questions for children and adolescents in American society. Such relationships, and the relative success or failure of individuals in managing them, are also much more explicitly and publicly documented than in most societies by the obligatory dating activities, in which even pre-pubertal children are expected to participate, and by the formal fraternities and sororities which form so important a part of the social context of adolescents and young adults. Finally, perhaps this enormous concern explains the huge number of studies of peer group relationships that continue to be carried out by American investigators, and in particular the many studies of popularity.

Societies also differ in the number and nature of the transition points with which they mark the developmental progress of the young. Much has been written about the social rites and ceremonies with

which non-Western societies have celebrated the entry into adulthood of young people, and about the confusion and the absence of
unambiguous markers in our own society. What does not seem to
have been much considered is the question of the transitions to which
present-day Western children and adolescents *are* subject. Yet such
transitions obviously exist, and seem likely to have an impact on the
peer group relationships of those concerned. It is statutory educational
provision which involves major changes at fixed chronological points
for all those who grow up in our society. Starting school at the age
of 5 probably means for all children an increase in the intensity of
peer group contact, and some change in its nature, even though the
degree of discontinuity is likely to be moderated by having attended
a pre-school group of some sort. The transition to secondary school,
usually at 11, must also alter peer group relationships. It seems likely
that where other children from the same junior school are present
in the secondary school class, the friendship group will for a time
consist of this little group. Nevertheless, adjustment must, even in
these cases, be made to new children, and ultimately a new set of
peer group relationships will have to be made. When it comes to
leaving school the situation is likely to be an untidy one, since some
adolescents will stay on as others leave; probably there will be much
less continuity in the friendship groups of those who leave early than
of those who stay on.

By the place it gives to the young, each society provides its own
distinctive arena within which children and adolescents meet and
interact with each other. In our own society, there seem to be four
main settings in which children's peer group relationships exist:
school, the family, semi-organized groups and the neighbourhood.
Of these, there is no question but that the school context has received
an overwhelming amount of research study time, at the expense of
the three others, and that, in particular, family settings for peer group
relationships have been hardly studied at all.

Studies of children's peer groups *within the context of school* can
perhaps be roughly categorized under two main headings: those concerned with the effects of aspects of school organization, and those
focusing on the relation between the peer group and the teacher. Of
the first kind of study, a number of different organizational features
have been examined. School size was the aspect studied by Willems
(1967) in an investigation of the degree to which this affected the
integration of academically marginal secondary-age pupils into the

social side of American school life. Another feature much studied by
British investigators is that of the streaming and setting practices of
schools, in so far as these affect the composition of pupils' friendship
groups. The large-scale investigation of Barker Lunn (1970) could
be cited here. Streaming practices were also one of many variables
which were looked at by Himmelweit and Swift (1970) in a study
of the immediate and long-term effects of a variety of school organizational features on the friendship groupings and social values of
secondary school boys. These authors found that features of schools,
such as selection of pupils and streaming, had significant effects on
pupil motivation, even offsetting the effects of family attitudes. It
seems fair to say that studies such as these have characteristically
shown, as one would expect, that the way school pupils are grouped
together and the attitudes which they encounter in the school do
produce an effect on the kinds of peer group relationships which they
establish.

When it comes to the investigation of the relation between pupils'
peer groups and the teacher the question arises of whether teachers
are aware of the friendship groupings of those they teach. Polansky
(1954) took a distinctive angle on this question by looking at the
degree to which teachers, in their interaction with pupils, supported
the status accorded by pupils to each other. A number of other
investigators have been interested in the extent to which teachers'
own perceptions of their pupils endorse or are at variance with the
perceptions that pupils have of each other. Nash (1973), for example,
compared the constructions of their pupils by Scottish junior school
teachers with the constructions of themselves by the pupils, and with
the friendship groupings they had formed; in both cases he found
a close relationship, suggesting that teacher perceptions are highly
salient for pupils in defining themselves and how they stand towards
other pupils. The same question has been a focus of interest, at the
secondary age level, for both Musgrove (1964) and Hargreaves
(1967). These investigators have been particularly concerned with
the discrepancy between teacher and pupil perceptions, and with
school situations where the peer group of pupils supports values which
are anti-academic and anti-teacher. This question has been taken a
step further in the work of Delamont (1976), which documents
through participant   observation the ongoing classroom interactions
in which pupils' peer group relationships can sometimes uphold and
sometimes undermine the teacher's effectiveness. Paul Willis's study

(1977) also provides a valuable insight into anti-school culture in a subgroup of adolescent boys.

While studies of the school context include an increasing number of investigations of classroom interaction, as yet no one seems to have looked at interaction in the playground, in the corridors or generally around the school environment. It is probably the case that the very character of such encounters which makes them so significant for peer group relationships – their spontaneity, fluidity and fast-flowing pace – is also what would create methodological difficulties in a study of them. Still, it is to be hoped that this aspect of the school context will be incorporated into future work.

A different kind of study, which cannot really be fitted into either of the two main categories suggested, is the small-scale investigation of Wooster and Harris (1972) into the effects of multiple changes of school. This study involved a comparison of the sons of British army personnel with a control group; the army boys had attended at least eight different schools because of their fathers' mobility. The degree to which these boys had achieved a coherent and stable view of themselves and other boys was found to be minimal, as compared with the controls; and Wooster and Harris concluded that the absence of a stable audience with whom to test out a developing view of oneself in relation to others had resulted in a greatly impaired ability to understand oneself and one's peers. Although this was a limited and essentially exploratory study, the results are suggestive in implying the possibly damaging effects on peer group relationships of high geographical mobility.

Very little can be said about the investigation of *families* as settings for children's peer groups, since this context has apparently not been studied at all in any systematic way. Nevertheless, the observations and impressions of the Newsons (1968) in their longitudinal study of 400 Nottingham children, suggest that this setting is important and significant in distinctive ways. One distinction to which these investigators draw attention is the degree to which parents actively involve themselves in the interactions between their own and other children. In some families, contact with peers is arranged by parents; in others, it is left to the children themselves. In some families, parents may try to direct their child's choice of friends, perhaps vetoing certain individuals. Again, some parents participate in the activities in which their child is engaged with others, or at least intervene in the case of trouble. According to the Newsons' own findings, such matters appear to be at least partly a function of the physical environment of the home, which make close supervision and involvement with children feasible or impossible. The degree to which parents are in fact active participants in the interactions between children does seem likely to affect the character of those interactions. And since children and adolescents do encounter each other within the setting of their own and each others' families, this context, and the ways in which it can differ, does not seem to deserve the neglect it has suffered.

The context of *leisure and activity groups* involving children has also not been extensively studied in relation to the peer group; though here one can at least cite certain studies. Those that have been carried out tend to have been of an earlier generation of research. The most obvious example is the work of the Sherifs (1964). In a series of studies these investigators looked at the ways in which stable social groupings gradually established themselves in a group of pre-adolescent boys on a camping holiday. Since the Sherifs were also interested in inter-group relationships, their studies incorporated an experiment in which conditions of inter-group rivalry and inter-group cooperation were deliberately introduced. The other major, and now classic, study of peer group relationships in a leisure activity setting is that of Lewin, Lippitt and White (1938). Here, three different leadership styles were adopted by an adult directing a group of pre-adolescent boys in a boat-building project. The activity of the boys was observed both during the leader's presence and when he was temporarily absent. It was found that only a democratic style of leadership succeeded in sustaining cheerful and purposeful activity, as well as cooperative peer group relations, in both conditions.

It is probably no accident that in both these studies adults took an important part in the children's peer group interactions. Sports clubs, activity or hobby groups, social clubs, guides or scouts – all these contexts tend to be set up for children by adults, and are often quite closely organized and supervised by adults. This point seems significant for three, related reasons. In the first place, the degree to which adults are directly involved is likely to alter the nature of the relationships between children or adolescents. Secondly, the fact that such contexts are adult-sponsored means that quite often the involvement of children in them, though nominally voluntary, may not be genuinely self-chosen. Finally, for precisely the same reason, many children and adolescents will choose not to become involved in such settings. This means that groups of children who are studied within this setting will not be representative of the general population.

The selectivity of the child population which comes within the context of leisure and activity groups also has a bearing on the type of child or adolescent to whom the next kind of setting – *the neigbourhood* – is relevant. Related to the fact that certain kinds of individual will and will not be drawn into leisure groups is the uneven distribution, across different kinds of social area, of leisure group facilities. This means that, in general, it will be the more socially deprived groups of children who are most involved in street culture. Since such groups are quite likely to be socially alienated, some kind of 'deviant' activity may be the currency of the peer groups established in these settings. If one adds to this the consideration that the places used as activity contexts by these kinds of young individuals are places officially set up for other kinds of purposes, it is hardly surprising that youthful peer groups in this setting are characteristically regarded as threats and nuisances by older groups, or that a mutual hostility develops. It seems understandable, therefore, that the studies of children's peer groups in the context of the neighbourhood have typically been of boys' gangs, delinquent or semi-delinquent in orientation. Two studies, one old and one more recent, will serve to illustrate the kinds of aspect which have usually been investigated. Thrasher's (1927) focus was on the structure of boys' gangs, and particularly on the power relationships within them. Similarly Patrick (1973), in his participant observation of delinquent gangs in Glasgow, looked at the degree of stability and the function of relationships within the gang, at inter-gang relationships, and at the part which various activities, especially fighting, played in achieving and maintaining group membership. Both these writers found, for instance, that gangs were typically quite highly organized. Somewhat at a tangent to these studies, but similarly concerned with group relationships and interactions, is the work of Labov (1972) on the street groups of American black youths. Again relying on participant observation, Labov has produced an analysis of characteristically complex social relationships, with the exclusion of certain individuals defined as 'lames', and of the elaborate and inventive forms of verbal interaction in such groups, largely consisting of ritual insults and the use of narrative.

In this section, literature on children's peer group relationship has been reviewed in terms of four distinct ecological settings: the school, the family, leisure groups and the neighbourhood. Some suggestions have been made about the differential social-psychological significance of each setting, and note has also been taken of the very uneven amount of empirical data which has been obtained so far within these four contexts.

The functions of the peer group

Questions about the function which the peer group may serve for children and adolescents concern two aspects: the phase of psychological development at which the group has its highest significance, and the kinds of significance which it holds. On the first kind of question, a number of writers have discussed the peer group in relation to the developmental period at which it is likely to be most important. Until recently there has been near-unanimity on the issue. Two writers, one who first put his case over two decades ago and one who is currently arguing a similar position, will serve to exemplify this widely accepted approach. From somewhat different points of view, both Erikson and Conger maintain that it is at adolescence that the peer group holds maximal significance. Erikson (1950), drawing on clinical and social-anthropological evidence, argues that adolescence provides a psychological moratorium necessary for the individual to try out new identities and to experiment with others before it is possible for him to establish himself socially, sexually and vocationally. In this experimentation, peers are vital, in exemplifying alternative identities, in providing moral support against the hostilities or incomprehension of adults, and in representing an arena in which possibilities can be safely tried out. More recently Conger (1973) puts a similar point of view from his own more academic background. Conger's argument rests on assumptions about sociological changes in our own society. The decline of the extended family, the institutionalized age segregation of the young, the delayed entry to adult society, and the expansion of communication networks among young people – all these features, Conger believes, have made for a greatly increased reliance on age-mates among adolescents.

Only relatively recently has this long-accepted view begun to be questioned. Hartup's comment has already been quoted in an earlier section of this chapter; the evidence, as he suggests, does not warrant the assumption that peers are any less important for young people before adolescence than during it. Conversely, the assumption of an overwhelming importance, at adolescence, on the part of the peer group is challenged in the recent study of Coleman (1974). In his study of British adolescents, Coleman found support for the view that the concerns of adolescents are essentially phasic and temporary and that what may be an issue at one stage of adolescence will, a little later, have been replaced by another kind of issue. Thus, although an adolescent girl may now be worrying about her friends, or about being in with the group, this worry may soon be dealt with and in its place she may be concerned with problems in her relationship with her parents – a concern that, in its turn, will eventually be resolved, to be replaced by some other, equally temporary concern. It may be, therefore, that a more complex view is needed of the relation between developmental stages and the significance of the peer group. The effect of social attitudes and practices, as Conger argues, must be important in influencing the nature of young people's relations with each other. But even in our own society, with its extreme consciousness of adolescents as a distinctive age-set, contacts do exist between adolescents and both older and younger people. And where pre-adolescents are concerned, the importance of other children, in all sorts of ways, should not be underestimated.

On the question of the kind of significance which the peer group holds for children and adolescents, there are, of course, links between the assumptions made and the view taken of developmental phases in which peers are specially important. This is probably why, again, Erikson has been one of the most influential spokesmen for certain widely held views. Erikson's name is perhaps most closely identified with two of the three main functions that have been put forward for the peer group: intimacy and consensual validation. The third function is the provision of a frame of reference. In Erikson's argument, the function of *intimacy* which peers can serve presupposes that the individual has already successfully negotiated a previous stage in which peers served to validate one's personal identity; without a firm sense of identity, Erikson suggests, intimacy is merely threatening. Among others who have emphasized intimacy as a function of peers is the neo-Freudian, Sullivan (1947). According to Sullivan, without the experience of a peer as an intimate – or chum, as Sullivan prefers it – an individual never overcomes personal insecurity. Among writers who stress this function on the basis of empirical research is Coleman (1974). Coleman's findings included evidence of a concern with personal loneliness and the absence of confidantes among a substantial number of his adolescent subjects.

It is certainly not accidental that those who emphasize intimacy characteristically refer to relationships with individuals rather than to a group of peers. Perhaps by its very definition, intimacy presupposes a close and relatively exclusive relationship with a chosen few. Conversely, the function of *validation by consensus* is usually seen as entailing groups rather than individuals; the support of one's own crowd is presumably more confirming than the support of one or two personal friends. Most writers, therefore, talk of the peer *group* in arguing this kind of function. Erikson, again, stresses the importance of the individual's peer group in validating his attempts at establishing a viable social identity. It is the group which is also stressed by Douvan and Adelson (1966) in their conclusion that peers provide a confirming experience for adolescents in their transition to a new identity. There is one writer, however, who relates this function to the context of encounters between pairs of friends. This is Duck (1973), whose research into friendship among adolescents and young adults focuses particularly on the function of consensual validation. As Duck sees it, close friends serve above all to confirm crucial but tentative personal beliefs, and hence, to validate each others' world view.

If the relation between the function of intimacy with individuals and consensual validation with groups seems easily justified, the linking of intimacy with girls and validation with boys is less self-evident. Yet this link runs through the writings and research of those interested in the peer group, from early investigators right up to the present day. Probably the main anchor for this traditional distinction is the argument put forward by Parsons (1955). Parsons maintained that in our society males and females faced a quite different task in acquiring their distinctive social roles. Because the nature of the female role was domestic and caretaking it was accessible to girls simply through their opportunities to witness their mothers at home. Boys, on the other hand, were unable to view the adult male role being played out, because of their exclusion from its occupational and leisure contexts. Thus boys, in order to experience being masculine, needed the context of a peer group of other boys; this provided necessary social support for modes of behaviour which were aimed at defining gender role. On their side, girls did not need such contexts since there was little ambiguity about the gender-linked behaviour they were trying to acquire. On the other hand, since the female role centred around expressive behaviour, girls required the experience of close and intimate relationships, first with same-sex and later with opposite-sex peers. Of many writers who have assumed the validity of this kind of assumption not many have justified it explicitly. One investigator who does so is Henry (1963). As always, Henry himself is worth quoting directly on this question. Here are his remarks on the abiding differences, as he sees them, between the sexes in terms of the relations with their peers:

> Little girls play with their dolls, their sewing, their cut-outs or their jacks, and their talk is not about rules of the game, but about the trivia of their semi-isolated play. And as they grow towards adolescence, girls do not need groups; as a matter of fact, for many of the things they do, more than two would be an obstacle. Boys flock; girls seldom get together in groups above four, whereas for boys a group of four is almost useless. Boys are dependent on masculine solidarity within a relatively large group. In boys' groups, the emphasis is on masculine unity; in girls' cliques the purpose is to shut out other girls.

This pen-picture may be an accurate portrayal of present-day Western, and specifically American society. Yet perhaps such a view ought to be regarded as having descriptive rather than explanatory value. In addition, sex roles are certainly changing and even now the relationship which any individual girl or boy has with friends and age-mates may be rather more complex than is implied by Henry's picture.

Rather less has been said about the third kind of function which it is sometimes assumed peers provide – the offering of a *frame of reference*. Here, those investigators who have viewed age-mates as sources of information in some sense seem to be putting this kind of case. For instance, Schofield (1965), in his large-scale survey of the attitudes of British adolescents towards sexuality, concluded that it was peers who, almost universally, represented the source of information for these young people as to the facts of human reproduction and the existence of various sexual practices. In Schofield's findings, the peer group was characteristically regarded as a reference source *faute de mieux*; but most studies which have focused on the reference function of peers have examined areas of experience in which peers are the preferred reference source. Of the many studies into conformity which compare responses to adult and peer group pressure, the work of Brittain (1968) is most explicit in defining the spheres in which peers, as against adults, are seen by children and adolescents as the natural authorities.

Conformity itself is, in fact, a traditional focus for assessing the kinds of function which peers hold for individual children, and to some extent it can be seen as the meeting point between all three functions discussed – intimacy, consensual validation and the provision of a frame of reference. Some mention has already been made of studies of peer group influence. In the main, the question has been one of the correlates of high and low yielding to peer influence. For example, Berenda (1950) investigated age differences in extent of conformity, while Wyer (1966) looked at sex differences; in terms of personality factors, a study by Kogan and Wallach (1966) will serve to illustrate this focus, and that of Lewis and Rosenblum (1975) to exemplify the interest in birth order effects. However, a number of criticisms may be made of the general line of such work. Many investigators have failed to distinguish between responses which indicate genuine conforming – that is, conversion on the part of the individual child – from those which merely represent outward compliance. Similarly important distinctions are frequently not made with respect to the nature of the task. For instance, an informational task can obviously not be equated with a normative one, although some investigators have generalized from only one kind of situation. Whether the peer norms themselves are unanimous or not, whether they are genuine or phoney, and whether they emanate from known peers or from an abstract nominal category of peers – all these features, clearly significant in influencing the nature of an individual's responses, are nevertheless frequently ignored in the design of conformity studies and the conclusions that are drawn from them.

Still more fundamentally, perhaps the model which underlies traditional studies of conforming to the peer group should itself be called into question. Implicit in this model is the assumption of an essentially fixed norm, in some sense represented by the group, to which the individual child is exposed, and to which he accedes or refuses to accede. What is omitted from such a view is the reciprocal nature of the influence which individuals have upon each other, and the fluid and created character of the beliefs and orientations operative at any moment within human groups, whether of adults or children. These features are apparent, however, in work such as the investigation of friendship pairs among adolescents by Duck (1973) who found that as friendships progressed mutual influences altered the outlooks of both individuals. Similarly, the classroom interaction studies of Delamont (1976) show how, in the flux of classroom events, the support by the pupils' group for individual cooperative or hostile encounters with the teacher ebbs and flows in a constantly changing sequence. A different perspective from the usual one towards the phenomenon of peer group conforming is also suggested by the results of a study by the present writer (Salmon, 1969). In this, orientation to the peer group was defined in terms of values, insight into peer group evaluative norms, assumed similarity to peers and conformity to peer norms; the subjects were junior school boys. Sociometric status in the classroom group of boys was used as a measure of current integration within the peer group. In an assessment of the relation between sociometric status and other indices, at the age of 8 and 10 years, it was found that sociometric status at 8 was highly correlated with peer group orientation at age 10, the association being stronger than that between status at age 8 and peer group orientation at age 8, or between status at age 10 and peer group orientation at age 10. What this rather complicated finding seems to suggest is that before real orientation to the peer group can occur, it is necessary already to have experienced personal integration within the group. It is presumably this experience of fairly prolonged intimacy with other individuals who help to define and live out the group norms which mediates familiarity with those norms and a personal identification with them. From this point of view, intimacy can be seen to be linked with the achievement of group consensus, and with the establishing and sharing of a frame of experiential reference in common with other peer group members.

Linked with the question of the functions of the peer group is the question of the reasons for, and the consequences of, high or low involvement with peers. Here the work which has already been outlined on the correlates of popularity and rejection is relevant, as, again, is that concerned with high or low peer group conformity. What does not seem to have received much attention, as yet, is the long-term effect of variations in relationships with peers during childhood. One study, however, seems to have a bearing on this issue. This is an investigation by Roff (1961) of the childhood peer group relationships of men discharged from American army service for misconduct or psychiatric invalidity. Roff's findings showed a marked impairment of such relationships – an impairment which he himself suggests provides an early diagnostic indicator of personality disorder. However, another interpretation is that the experience during childhood of isolation from other children or rejection by them is itself a personally damaging heritage, and that its consequences would be particularly likely to re-emerge within the essentially peer group setting of service army life.

Similarly neglected is the question of the precise ways in which peer relationships are distinctive. In particular, the differences between such relationships and those with siblings seem important, as does the question of the relative separation or integration between the two.

Intimacy, consensus, and the provision of a frame of reference – these seem to have formed the main themes among theorists and investigators who have considered questions of the functions of peer group relationships. The bias, already mentioned, with respect to age and gender in the study of children's peer groups can ultimately be traced back to the theoretical assumptions that have characteristically been adopted in this sphere. Here again, however, some aspects of the received wisdom may be questioned, as may the neglect of particular issues in relation to the function of peers.

The developmental significance of peer group relationships

It is perhaps impossible to do justice to the question of the functions which the peer group may serve for individuals without considering the ways in which relationships with peers affect psychological development. Relatively few writers, however, have addressed themselves explicitly to this issue. Of those already mentioned, Erikson is probably the sole exemplar of such an interest; his theory is essentially a developmental one, and the two phases at which peers are seen as maximally salient – early and late adolescence – involve crises of identity and intimacy, the solution to which forwards the individual's psychosocial development. It seems also that the findings of the Roff study (see p. 114) have possible implications for developmental questions in suggesting that impairment of peer relations during childhood may result in personal difficulties during adult life.

The developmental significance of peer group relationships does, however, play a central part in the account which Piaget gives of children's interactions (1928). This significance, as Piaget views it, lies in mediating the concepts of reciprocity and mutuality which underlie a morality of co-operation rather than constraint. The evidence on which Piaget himself has drawn for this view is derived from children's talk about moral issues and imperatives, and from observations of children playing rule-governed games. A rather more process-focused kind of evidence for the Piagetian perspective has been gathered by Flavell (Flavell et al., 1968) in a series of investigations of the role-taking and empathic skills of children. In general such evidence strongly supports Piaget's case that children, through establishing relationships of equality with other children, are enabled to take the perspective of the other. On the same line of argument some recent work by Light (1977) is worth mentioning. This work, which has involved assessing the relation between the perspective-taking skills of pre-school children and the nature of their relationships with their mothers, indicates that these kinds of social skills seem to be a function of mother-child relationships which stress symmetry rather than maternal dominance. If this kind of finding is upheld in further work, it suggests that the importance, developmentally, of peer relationships may lie in their typically equal character. This equality, however, though characteristic is not exclusive to such relationships.

One theoretical position which seems to promise a potentially fruitful view of the developmental importance of peer group relationship is that of symbolic interactionism. This is because the concepts of socially constructed and socially shared meanings central to this theory seem applicable par excellence to the arena of the encounters between children. Only one writer, however, seems to have explored the implications of this approach for the understanding of peer group relationships. This is Weinstein (1973) who, in an essay on the significance which children may hold for each other, speculates that the relative equality of power relationships may facilitate the development of social strategies which could never have been learned in the more unequal relationships with adults. In particular, Weinstein suggests, the greater control which children have over outcomes in child–child as against child–adult relationships enables them to engage in characteristically experimental kinds of manoeuvres, and to receive unambiguous feedback in their encounters with their peers. Peer group relationships, in Weinstein's view, also offer multiple opportunities for witnessing the social strategies of others, and seeing how far these are effective; this may be particularly important for learning how to manage relationships with older and younger children, and especially for learning how to avoid being exploited by older ones. Finally, they provide an arena for learning self-presentation and the ability to account, intelligibly, for one's actions.

Rather similar to the symbolic interactionist position is that of the ethnomethodologists. Here, again, the attention of writers is characteristically on adults rather than children; but an exception is Speier (1970). Speier, writing about the everyday world of children, draws attention to the complexity and subtlety of the interactional competencies of even quite young children, as seen, for example, in the sophistication of a child's understanding of the names to be used when talking to and about the members of a friend's family. Speier's suggestions for a study of children's peer group relationships, from an ethnomethodological point of view, seem worth quoting here:

> Where childhood social organization is concerned, the analysis would focus on children's conversational turn-taking and such co-ordinated phenomena as questions and answers, utterance completion units, interruptions and jointly produced utterances. How do children manage their methodical participation in these co-ordinated conversational productions? How do they utilize some of these conversational resources in the performance of routines like house calls, street contacts, greeting and summoning, leave-taking, topically eventful talk, play and game categorization practices, insulting, arguing, introduction, initiating conversation with adults, and so forth? (1970, 217)

A final theoretical perspective which deserves some consideration in this sphere is that of personal construct theory (Kelly, 1955). Again, it must be said that no-one as yet has systematically applied this perspective to the relationships between children or adolescents. But Kelly's concepts of commonality and sociality seem highly relevant to such relationships, and to the significance of these relationships in facilitating social development. In so far as the encounters between children depend upon the development and elaboration of shared construing, and upon mutual understanding of how the other sees things, these concepts may be crucial in defining the way in which peer relationships both constitute, in themselves, an experience of genuinely social relating to others, and lay the framework for future social relationships.

Little work has been devoted as yet to the issue of the specifically developmental significance of peer group relationships. However, the work of Piaget and Flavell seems seminal; and the concepts of the symbolic interactionist and ethnomethodological school seem potentially fruitful, as does the approach of personal construct theory.

Summary

In this chapter, work on the role of the peer group during childhood and adolescence has been analysed in terms of the common assumptive ground which it seems to reveal. Many of these common assumptions are, it has been suggested, open to question. In particular, criticism has been directed at the somewhat ethnocentric view which has resulted in a neglect of cultural relativism and differences of social setting, as well as a characteristically static and limited view of the nature of children's peer groups. New directions in focus and methodology do, however, seem to be emerging, and the concepts of several currently influential theoretical schools seem at least potentially fruitful for an understanding of this developmental area.

References

Ariés, P. (1962) *Centuries of Childhood*. New York: Vintage Books.

Barker Lunn, J. C. (1970) *Streaming in the Primary School*. Slough: National Foundation for Educational Research.

Berenda, R. W. (1950) *The Influence of the Group on the Judgments of Children*. New York: King's Crown Press.

Brittain, C. B. (1968) An exploration of the bases of peer-compliance and parent-compliance in adolescence. *Adolescence 2*: 445–58.

Bronfenbrenner, U. (1970) *Two Worlds of Childhood*. New York: Russell Sage Foundation.

Cavior, N. and Dokecki, P. R. (1973) Physical attractiveness, perceived attitude similarity and academic achievement as contributors to interpersonal attraction among adolescents. *Developmental Psychology 9*: 44–54.

Charlesworth R. and Hartup, W. W. (1967) Positive social reinforcement in the nursery school peer group. *Child Development 38*: 993–1002.

Coleman, J. C. (1974) *Relationships in Adolescence*. London: Routledge and Kegan Paul.

Coleman, J. C. (1978) Current contradictions in adolescent theory. *Journal of Youth and Adolescence 7*: 1–11.

Coleman, J. S. (1961) *The Adolescent Society*. New York: Free Press.

Conger, J. J. (1973) *Adolescence and Youth: Psychological Development in a Changing World*. New York: Harper and Row.

Costanzo, P. R. (1970) Conformity development as a function of self-blame. *Journal of Personality and Social Psychology 14*: 366–74.

Delamont, S. (1976) Beyond Flanders' Fields: the relationship of subject-matter and individuality to classroom style. In M. Stubbs and S. Delamont (eds) *Explorations in Classroom Observation*. Chichester: John Wiley.

Douvan, E. and Adelson, J. (1966) *The Adolescent Experience*. New York: John Wiley.

Duck, S. W. (1973) Similarity and perceived similarity of personal constructs as influences on friendship choice. *British Journal of Social and Clinical Psychology 12*: 1–6.

Dunphy, D. C. (1972) Peer group socialization. In F. J. Hunt (ed.) *Socialization in Australia*. Sydney: Angus and Robertson.

Erikson, E. H. (1950) *Childhood and Society*. New York: Norton.

Flavell, J. H., Botkin, P. T., Fry, C. L., Wright, J. W. and Jarvis, P. E. (1968) *The Development of Role-Taking and Communication Skills in Children*. New York: John Wiley.

Freud, A. and Dann, S. (1951) An experiment in group upbringing. In R. Eisler et al. (eds) *The Psychoanalytic Study of the Child 6*. New York: International Universities Press.

Hare, A. P. (1952) A study of interaction and consensus in different sized groups. *American Sociological Review 17*: 261–7.

Hargreaves, D. H. (1967) *Social Relations in a Secondary School*. London: Routledge and Kegan Paul.

Hartup, W. W. (1970) Peer interaction and social organization. In P. H. Mussen (ed.) *Carmichael's Manual of Child Psychology*. New York: John Wiley.

Harvey, O. J. and Rutherford, J. (1960) Status in the informal group: influence and influenceability at differing age levels. *Child Development 31*: 377–85.

Henry, J. (1963) *Culture against Man*. New York: Random House.

Himmelweit, H. and Swift, B. (1970) A model for the understanding of school as a socializing agent. In P. H. Mussen, J. Langer and M. Covington (eds) *Trends and Issues in Developmental Psychology*. New York: Holt, Rinehart and Winston.

Horowitz, H. (1967) Predictions of adolescent popularity and rejection from achievement and interests tests. *Journal of Educational Psychology 58*: 170–4.

Jones, M. C. (1958) Psychological correlates of somatic development *Child Development 36*: 899–911.

Kelly, G. A. (1955) *The Psychology of Personal Constructs*. New York: Norton.

Kogan, N. and Wallach, M. A. (1966) Modification of a judgmental style through group interaction. *Journal of Personality and Social Psychology 4*: 165–74.

Labov, W. (1972) The logic of non-standard English. In P. H. Mussen, J. J. Conger and J. Kagan (eds) *Basic and Contemporary Issues in Developmental Psychology*. New York: Harper and Row.

Lewin, K., Lippitt, R. and White, R. K. (1938) Patterns of aggressive behaviour in experimentally created 'social climates'. *Journal of Social Psychology 10*: 271–99.

Lewis, M. and Rosenblum, L. (eds) (1975) *Friendship and Peer Relations*. New York: John Wiley.

Light, P. H. (1977) Social role-taking in four-year-olds. Paper presented to British Psychological Society Developmental and Educational Sections' Joint Annual Conference, Cambridge.

Miller, D. R. and Swanson, G. E. (1958) *The Changing American Parent.* New York: John Wiley.

Musgrove, F. (1964) *Youth and the Social Order.* London: Routledge and Kegan Paul.

Nash, R. (1973) *Classrooms Observed.* London: Routledge and Kegan Paul.

Newson, J. and Newson, E. (1968) *Four Years Old in an Urban Community.* London: Allen and Unwin.

Northway, M. L. (1943) Social relationships among pre-school children' abstracts and interpretations of three studies. *Sociometry 6*: 429–33.

Parsons, T. and Bales, R. F. (1955) *Family, Socialization and Interaction Process.* Glencoe: Illinios Free Press.

Parten, M. B. (1933) Social participation among pre-school children. *Journal of Abnormal and Social Psychology 27*: 243–69.

Patrick, J. (1973) *A Glasgow Gang Observed.* London: Eyre Methuen.

Peck, R. F. (1958) Family patterns correlated with adolescent personality structure. *Journal of Abnormal and Social Psychology 47*: 347–50.

Piaget, J. (1928) *The Moral Judgment of the Child.* London: Kegan Paul.

Polansky, N. (1954) Group social climate and teachers' supportiveness of group status systems. *Journal of Educational Sociology 28*: 115–23.

Riesman, D. (1950) *The Lonely Crowd.* New Haven, Connecticut: Yale University Press.

Roff, M. (1961) Childhood social interaction and young adult bad conduct *Journal of Abnormal and Social Psychology 63*: 333–7.

Salmon, P. (1969) Differential conforming as a developmental process. *British Journal of Social and Clinical Psychology 8*: 22–31.

Schofield, M. (1965) *The Sexual Behaviour of Young People.* London: Longmans

Sherif, M. and Sherif, C. (1964) *Reference Groups.* New York: Harper and Row.

Smith, A. J. (1960) A developmental study of group processes. *Journal of Genetic Psychology 97*: 29–30.

Speier, M. (1970) The everyday world of the child. In J. D. Douglas (ed.) *Understanding Everyday Life.* New York: Aldine Publishing Company.

Stubbs, M. and Delamont, S. (1976) *Explorations in Classroom Observation.* Chichester: John Wiley.

Sturt, R. (1976) Unpublished thesis, Diploma in Child Development, University of London Institute of Education.

Sullivan, H. S. (1947) *Conceptions of Modern Psychiatry.* New York: Norton.

Thrasher, F. M. (1927) *The Gang.* Chicago: University of Chicago Press.

Upson, P. (1975) Adolescents and groups, subcultures and counter-cultures In S. Meyerson (ed.) *Adolescence: The Crises of Adjustment.* London: Allen and Unwin.

Walker, R. and Adelman, C. (1976) Strawberries. In M. Stubbs and S Delamont (eds) *Explorations in Classroom Observation.* Chichester: John Wiley.

Weinstein, E. A. (1973) The development of interpersonal competence. In

D. A. Goslin (ed.) *Handbook of Socialization Theory and Research*. New York: Rand McNally.

Wheeler, D. K. (1961) Popularity among adolescents in Western Australia and in the United States of America. *The School Review 49*: 67–81.

Willems, E. P. (1967) Sense of obligation to high school activities as related to school size and marginality of student. *Child Development 38*: 1247–60.

Willis, Paul (1977) *Learning to Labour*. Farnborough: Saxon House.

Wooster, A. D. and Harris, G. (1972) Concepts of self and others in highly mobile service boys. *Educational Research 12*: 46–52.

Wyer, R. S. (1966) Effects of incentive to perform well, group attraction, and group acceptance on conformity in a judgmental task. *Journal of Personality and Social Psychology 4*: 21–6.

6   The home and the school

Ronald Davie

The influence of the home and the family upon children's development in most of its facets is very powerful. The environmental influences at work are sometimes subtle and complex, at other times they are simpler and more obvious; sometimes they are idiosyncratic, even unique, whilst at other times they echo local, subcultural or national norms, values and ideologies. The influence of the school on the other hand is not only almost certainly less powerful but is also more difficult to establish. As we shall see later, this is due in part to the fact that there is much greater variability between home environments than between school environments.

There are many ways of studying these influences. One important continuum in this regard is the scale of the enquiry, i.e. the size of the sample used. A closely related feature is the sophistication of the measures used. Thus at one extreme we may find a national or large-scale study using such variables as socio-economic status, family size, type of school and IQ. At the other extreme lie studies of individual schools, small groups of pupils or small samples of families and children using, for example, observational techniques or detailed interviews. For the individual researcher or team these are usually alternative strategies but in terms of the advancement of our understanding they are essentially complementary.

The fact that the major emphasis of the present chapter is upon large-scale enquiries should therefore not be taken to imply that these are judged to be of greater intrinsic or relative value. Rather, it reflects to some extent the field of interest and past experience of the author. In addition, it was seen as giving a certain unity to the chapter and of exploring a range of concepts, techniques and findings which in general tend to be neglected in many text books of psychology.

Socio-economic status and educational performance

Socio-economic status may be conceptualized and measured or assessed in a variety of ways. Most researchers in the educational, medical and social fields use the term to denote an individual's (or family's) position on a hierarchical continuum defined in terms of variables like occupational skill or status, housing, level of formal education and income. The assumption is normally made that such parameters are indirectly linked to the socialization process and to less tangible characteristics of individuals and families such as norms of behaviour, values, educational and vocational aspirations and standards of health care. Indeed, there is a considerable amount of evidence to indicate that this is so (Zigler, 1970).

In Britain, the most frequently used index of socio-economic status is the Registrar General's classification of occupations ('social class') which for families is based upon the occupation of the male head of the household. In the US, probably because of greater social and cultural heterogeneity and social mobility, a single variable like occupation is seldom felt to be satisfactory and some composite index is used (Havighurst, 1971).

However, in both countries, the evidence for a strong relationship between the socio-economic status of the family and the educational attainments of its children is unequivocal. For example, in a longitudinal study of a complete week's births in Britain, some 16,000 in all, marked social class differences were found in educational attainments at age seven and eleven years (Davie et al., 1972; Davie, 1973). The results from a reading test given to the children at the age of seven are reproduced in Table 6.1.

The trend in these results from social class I (higher professional occupations) through to social class V (unskilled occupations) is highly significant statistically ($p < \cdot001$). Later, longitudinal analysis of results for this same cohort of children revealed that the social class differences in reading attainment had widened over the period from

Table 6.1   Reading test score by social class. National Child Development study of seven-year-olds

Reading test score	Social class groups						
	I	*II*	*III (non-manual)*	*III (manual)*	*IV*	*V*	*Total*
	%	%	%	%	%	%	%
0–20	8·2	14·7	13·9	30·4	37·2	48·3	28·6
21–28	37·5	38·8	43·1	41·0	37·9	34·3	39·3
29–30	54·3	46·6	43·0	28·7	25·0	17·3	32·1
Total	100·0	100·1	100·0	100·1	100·1	99·9	100·0

From Davie et al. (1972)

seven to eleven years of age (Fogelman and Goldstein, 1976). The relationship between social class and educational progress was demonstrated in an earlier British national cohort (Douglas, 1967; Douglas et al., 1968) and has emerged in a number of locally based but influential studies (e.g. Floud et al., 1956; Fraser, 1959). Coleman et al. (1966) in a frequently cited report showed amongst other things the extent to which aspects of the home environment – including the socio-economic – are strongly related to children's educational progress in American schools.

The value of socio-economic status as an independent variable for the educational researcher derives in large measure from its power as a predictor of educational attainment and of other relevant dependent variables such as behaviour and adjustment in school. When used in this way it is not seen as a causal factor but rather as a variable known to be associated with aspects of the home environment which may be causally linked to attainment (e.g. parental attitudes, behaviour, use of language) as well as with other aspects which, although correlated with attainment, can have no direct causal links (e.g. housing, family size). Socio-economic status may also be associated with genetic differences. It is, then, a rather crude 'compendium variable' reflecting a wide range of direct and indirect influences centred upon the family. Furthermore, when assessed correctly, it is a measure with high reliability.

The inclusion of socio-economic status in an analysis where the principal focus of attention is overtly on circumstances outside the home (e.g. regional differences, urban/rural location, type of schooling) may serve to show that part, or even all, of the variance thought to be associated with such external factors can be accounted for by differences between families. Similarly, when the major interest is in the relationship between children's attainment and factors centred upon the home, the inclusion of socio-economic status as an independent variable may throw useful light upon the extent to which variance thought to be attributable to such factors is being accounted for.

Such disagreement as has arisen about the relevance and value of socio-economic status as a variable in this general context seem to be due to misunderstandings or misinterpretations, as is often the case in such controversies. Jackson and Marsden (1962), for example, assert that schools are middle-class institutions with middle-class values and norms of behaviour, which discriminate against working class children. It is clear that these authors are not using the terms 'middle class' as most British researchers would, i.e. merely to identify individuals or families as belonging to the non-manual occupational group. Otherwise the description of schools as middle-class institutions is redundant in that all teachers must by definition be middle-class. Jackson and Marsden were expressing – in a rather more contentious form – what Davie et al. (1972, pp. 28–9) commented upon as follows: 'To the extent that the school and the individual teachers have certain standards, certain values and certain priorities, a child who tends to conform to these norms will be seen as "progressing satisfactorily". Such a child is more likely to come from a middle-class home; he is, as it were, on the same wavelength.' These latter authors go on to point out that even the more objective yardsticks of educational progress – examination results and standardized tests of attainment – reflect what their users judge to be desirable skills, abilities or knowledge. The values and priorities inherent in such judgements are rarely made explicit but they are certainly not absolute or culture-free. Furthermore, they are more commonly met in middle-class homes than in others.

We shall return to this point in a later section. However, it is interesting to note here that Wiseman (1972) – one of the critics of the use of social class – in discussing Jackson and Marsden's thesis (1962) appears at one point to agree, when he talks of 'many teachers' being 'consciously or unconsciously, uncompromisingly hostile to these more alien (i.e. working class) cultures'. However, shortly afterwards he says that, 'Those of us with experience in teacher-training find little correlation between socio-political attitudes or social class on the one hand and progressive educational methods on the other'. He thus seems to misunderstand the authors' major point that over and above any hostility or any socio-political attitudes, the system itself – almost inevitably it seems – embodies certain implicit values, which some groups in the population share and which other groups at best find unfamiliar and more difficult to understand and to accept.

In summary, then, there can be no valid objection to the use of socio-economic status, or social class, in a research context provided its limitations are understood by the researcher and later conveyed to his readers. However, if the interpretation of the results include the use of status or class in a wider context, when broader social, even political, attitudes come nearer to the surface of the discussion, there is a clear danger that the borderline between questions of fact and questions of opinion may not be drawn clearly enough.

The relevance of material circumstances

Just as with socio-economic status, it is difficult to conceive of any direct, or causal, link between the material conditions in which a child and family live and the child's progress in school. However, in fairly obvious ways, some causal connections may not be difficult to postulate. Thus, if beds have to be shared, particularly by children of different ages, there is more likely to be disturbance of sleep with some consequent reduction in mental alertness or drive in school. Limited space and insufficient heating of accommodation may create conditions which are unconducive to any kind of sustained concentration in the home. This may not only affect older children's ability or readiness to carry out homework assignments but in a more general way may tend to inhibit any member of the family from engaging in activities which are best done in reasonable comfort and without undue interruption, e.g. reading a book, writing a letter or essay. Thus, younger children raised in such an atmosphere are less likely to enter school able to read and may see little point in acquiring this skill.

We have already moved from considering causal links, where the connection between school progress and material circumstances in the home may be quite close and specific (e.g. with sleep disturbance and homework), to more tenuous and speculative relationships. It is true that a number of researchers have established correlations between children's level of attainment and the literacy level in the home; and we shall discuss these in the following section on cultural factors in the home. However, the causal link between, say, inadequate accommodation and the number of books in the house is impossible to establish without a controlled experiment.

Another well established correlation is that between family size (i.e., number of children in the family, or household) and many aspects of children's development including school attainment. Davie et al. (1972), for example, showed that at the age of seven years the 'effects' of family size are quite substantial in terms of reading attainment and of social adjustment in school. The size of such 'effects', of course, depends not only upon how family size is assessed (whether step-siblings are included, etc.) but also upon precisely how it is used in any analysis. For example, it may be entered into an analysis as a continuous variable or as a grouped variable (e.g. small, medium and large families). If this latter strategy is adopted, the number of groups and their definition is likely to affect the outcome, as is the number and nature of any other independent variables included in the analysis. Davie et al. (1972) introduced yet another variation by examining separately the 'effects' upon their study children of the number of younger siblings and of older ones. Using a reading test as the dependent variable, grouping the two assessments of family size and also including social class, sex, birth weight, maternal age and maternal smoking during pregnancy in a regression analysis, they found that the 'effect' of the number of older siblings upon reading attainment was about twice as large as that of younger siblings. The combined 'effect' of both these measures of family size in this analysis was substantially more than social class and was equivalent to a difference in reading age of about 24 months (at age seven).

Further analysis of the same cohort of children in this longitudinal study showed that family size was exerting a continuing 'effect' between the ages of seven and eleven years (Fogelman and Goldstein, 1976) contrary to the earlier findings of Douglas (1967).

The use of the word 'effect' in quotation marks is intended here and elsewhere in this chapter to serve as a reminder that a direct, causal relationship is not implied. An explanation for family size differences which has been advanced is that children in large families tend to have less contact with their parents and other adults than do their peers in small families. This may mean that their verbal skills and concepts and social skills are slower to develop, or are permanently affected to some degree, which in turn would disadvantage them in a variety of learning and social situations – including school. In addition, there will tend to be differences in family income and in housing between families of different size so that there may be important differences in life style. Finally, family size may be related to the priorities which parents have for themselves and for their children.

The correlation between limited accommodation (i.e. overcrowding) and children's development has been well documented and, as we have seen above, some speculative reasons are not difficult to find. That these reasons cannot be a sufficient explanation is evidenced by the finding that, on average, Scottish children live in the most overcrowded conditions in Britain, and yet they are better readers than their English and Welsh counterparts, at least during the primary school years (Davie et al., op. cit.). The correlations between household amenities (e.g. use of bathroom, indoor toilet) and children's attainments are perhaps even more puzzling. It is quite possible that these relationships can be entirely explained in terms of other readily measurable variables such as income, overcrowding, socio-economic status, family size, etc., although attempts to do this (e.g. Davie et al., 1972; Peaker, 1967) have not been successful.

It is also possible that in some measure household amenities exert their 'effect' on children's attainments through parents' attitudes and behaviour. Indeed Peaker's analysis suggests as much. However, even if valid, this still leaves open the question as to the processes involved. Is it simply that, as poorly housed families become better housed, the parents' attitudes towards education and their aspirations for their children tend to shift towards those of families who already have better housing? When the question is posed in this form, it virtually invites a negative response, since changes in human behaviour may be lots of things but they are rarely simple! It is at least possible – some would say likely – that the shift in parental attitudes, or the potential for such a shift, in some measure *precedes* the improvement in material circumstances, so that the latter can be seen as a sequel of a drive towards upward social mobility.

Cultural factors in the home

When examining directly the relationships between the life style of the family, the parents' attitudes, their behaviour towards their children and towards outside agencies such as schools, we seem to be on firmer ground. The causal links are easier to postulate; they are more plausible; they fit more readily into theoretical models. However, the causal factors may be more apparent than real; the researcher (and the reader) must be alert to the possibility that his own cultural perspective and his own value judgements are prejudicing the outcome of his analyses and his interpretations.

We have already pointed to the fact that the choice of a dependent variable reflects a value judgement. This is more subtle than is sometimes realized. For example, the choice of a reading test score as a yardstick may be uncontroversial in that we can all agree – at least at this point in the history of human development – that literacy is highly desirable for all children. Nevertheless, when we come to select a particular test a difficulty arises. Leaving aside the problem of whether to test recognition or understanding of the printed word, we find that virtually all available reading tests have been developed by individuals from particular social groups, who have furthermore been successful in the present educational system. The vocabulary they use in the test items will tend to reflect this background. The final selection of items for the test will be based upon their facility value and upon their capacity to discriminate between good and poor readers. Good readers will to an extent tend to be those children who have successfully mastered the skills of reading in the context of reading materials and a learning situation which broadly mirror the values and vocabulary of the social groups to which the test constructors (and researchers) belong.

We can, of course, overemphasize the limitations of this process but it is not difficult to spot the possible circularity of conclusions which may flow from the apparently unexceptionable choice of literacy as a dependant variable. With a variable such as social adjustment in school, which even more directly reflects the norms and values of schools and the social groups from which teachers and researchers are drawn, the possibility of an unintentionally prejudiced outcome to our analyses and interpretations seems more real.

The best known British studies in the past two decades or so, which have investigated the relationships between cultural factors in the home and children's educational progress include those by Fraser (1959); Douglas (1967); Douglas, et al. (1968); Peaker (1967) and Davie et al. (1972). Fraser in a study of 400 Aberdeen schoolchildren

looked in some detail at the home environment to assess 'whether environmental factors were related to school progress in greater degree
than one might expect as a result of the common factor of intelligence'.
Fraser was able to show that her composite index of the home environment was more closely associated with educational attainments than
with measured IQ, although it is important to emphasize in passing
that there was a significant correlation between home environment
and the latter. The implicit question is often posed in a research context: other things (including IQ) being equal, what is the relationship
between home environment and educational attainment? Of course,
we accept that in the real world other things are not equal. However,
sometimes insufficient weight is given to the likelihood that some of
the inequalities that we partial out in our analyses (and notably IQ)
may be influenced by the home environment in ways which may not
differ substantially from the ways in which environmental factors
affect school progress. Thus, our quantitative assessment of the
'importance' of the home environment for school progress may
represent a considerable underestimate of its real importance.

Among the environmental components which made up Fraser's
composite index were parental attitudes both to their children's education and to their future occupations. Douglas and his colleagues
(1968) reinforced this finding. The results of their statistical analyses
indicated that overt parental interest in their children's education
accounted for more of the variance in school performance than size
of family, the 'standard of the home' or the standard of the school,
as evidenced by its academic record. The publication of the Plowden
Report and in particular the analysis by Peaker (1967) of data from
a national survey further strengthened this conclusion. However,
Peaker went on to caution with particular regard to parental attitudes to their children's education that it is impossible in a cor-
relational study to know which is cause and which is effect. This is
especially important when attempting to interpret the evidence on
the relative weight of various independent variables in such analyses.
Whereas it is possible that a child's progress in school may affect the
level of his parents' interest, it is most unlikely that such progress
will influence either the material circumstances of the home or the
academic record of the school as a whole.

Despite Peaker's cautionary note, his results have been widely
referred to as showing that parental attitudes to education are more
important for children's progress at school than either the quality

of the schooling or the circumstances of the family. Apart from the cause-effect difficulty mentioned above, there is a special problem in assessing parental interest validly. If teachers' ratings are used there is the danger that their judgements may be based on inferences from children's appearance, behaviour, speech or educational attainments, or from parents' appearance, behaviour or speech. If a more objective yardstick is used, such as parental visits to school, there is the certainty that some parents' failure to visit may be attributable to factors other than interest in their child's education. Banks and Finlayson (1973), for example, looking in more depth at parental values and attitudes, found very few parents who were uninterested in their children's schooling, yet the cruder measures outlined above yield a substantial minority.

This is not to say that Peaker's analysis is invalid nor that parental interest is unimportant, but in all studies, especially perhaps in large-scale surveys, the relative crudity of the basic data should not be overlooked, however sophisticated that statistical analysis. Goldstein (1972, 1976) has been critical of Peaker's and similar analyses and the interpretation of such findings on other grounds. Apart from purely statistical considerations, Goldstein points out that if we 'wish to make statements about the relative "importance" of different factors (in a regression analysis) we need to specify the utilities or costs to be attached to any given test score'. He continues: 'to assume implicitly that the utilities are proportional to sums of squared deviations from a mean value ... is quite arbitrary and without a particular educational justification'. This underlines the necessity of specifying any assumptions made in such analyses so that others are aware of their possible implications for the interpretation of results.

No consideration of cultural factors in the home in relation to schooling could be complete without some reference to the very considerable influence of Bernstein's writing on this topic. There have been two major strands in his work: the research into socio-linguistic codes and the research into education as an agency of social control. He has frequently been misunderstood and his ideas oversimplified, which is not altogether surprising since his prose is tightly packed and often difficult to follow. Bernstein's earliest work (1959, 1960), for which he is still best known, was his distinction between public and formal language usage, which he described, respectively, as 'restricted' and 'elaborated' codes. The former was characterized by 'short grammatical, simple, often unfinished sentences, a poor syntactical structure stressing the active mood', whilst the latter was language where 'accurate grammatical order and syntax regulates what is said'. He linked the use of these two codes with working-class and middle-class speech and provoked a hostile reaction from, for example, Labov (1970) and Ginsburg (1972). We shall return to this controversy later. In the present context the significant aspect of Bernstein's work is his linking of the use of the elaborated code with schools, and the disadvantage of working-class children in such a situation. However, Bernstein eschews the concept of the 'disadvantaged child', as we shall see later, and since the early 1960s has been more concerned with analysing role systems, communication and social control within the family on the one hand and on the other hand the organizational structure of schools and the contents or curricula of education. He uses the term 'classification' to describe the boundaries between areas of educational knowledge. Where it is 'strong', these areas are well insulated from each other and where it is 'weak' the boundaries are more fluid. The term 'frame' is used to describe 'the degree of control teacher and pupil possess over the selection, organization and pacing of the knowledge transmitted and received in the pedagogical relationship'.

In Bernstein's view (1973), then, the factors in the home which are of particular relevance educationally and socially are those which have to do with the nature of the roles adopted by members of the family, the way in which they communicate with each other and the forms of social control adopted. Their relevance educationally is that they interact with the strength of the classification and framing in the school. He now makes clear that elaborated codes are not *necessarily* 'middle-class communication procedures' nor does their use *necessarily* disadvantage working class or promulgate class structures. However, they may do so to the extent that the classification and framing which control their transmission in formal education are strong. With weak classification and framing, the content of education becomes more fluid, the range of options for its transmission become wider and the codes become more integrated with each other.

Children of atypical families

An atypical family is difficult to define except in very general or else in operational terms. However, in this section we shall mostly be concerned with family situations which affect relatively small proportions of children and which might be regarded as having potentially adverse effects.

It hardly needs saying that few – if any – situations inevitably produce harmful results. This may be partly because children vary a great deal in their resilience in the face of disturbance or disruption of normal patterns of upbringing. Partly, too, family situations which overtly present similar features may vary a great deal in the many, often subtle, interactions through which the effects upon children are transmitted. It must be said at the outset that we know very little as yet about the nature of these processes.

One definition of an atypical family is a family where the parents are not both the natural, or biological, parents of the children. Pringle et al. (1966) carried out some comparisons between the reading attainment of seven-year-olds living with both natural parents and those in atypical families in a large, British, national study. Straightforward comparisons revealed that the children in atypical families as a group had poorer reading test scores. However, since there was a significant tendency for atypical family situations to occur more frequently in lower social class groups the comparisons were repeated within social class groups. This second analysis showed similar results in social classes I, II and III but in social classes IV and V there were now no significant differences. The authors speculated whether an atypical situation was more readily accepted in the two lower social class groups so that any adverse affects were minimized. Alternatively, they wondered whether the children in these latter groups were disadvantaged in so many other respects that any adverse effects of an atypical family situation were masked.

One sub-category of children in atypical family situations in the above sense contains those whose parents have divorced. Douglas (1970) and Rutter (1971; 1975) have concluded that children's behaviour tends to be adversely affected not by the divorce itself but by the marital tension and poor family relationships which precede the divorce. George and Wilding (1972) investigating the subsequent educational progress of children in motherless families, where the fathers were separated or divorced, found that there was thought to be some educational deterioration in 20 per cent of cases. However, in a further 21 per cent of the children there was judged to be some educational improvement.

Another sub-category within this general framework is of children in one-parent families. Ferri (1976) found that about one child in twenty in Britain by the age of eleven was living in a one-parent family; the ratio of fatherless to motherless families was about six to one. As one might predict, the measurable effects on children varied with the particular circumstances (e.g. separation, divorce, bereavement, illegitimacy). However, where the one-parent status was accompanied by low income and poor housing, as was often the case in fatherless families, the educational disadvantage was marked.

Adoptive parents are, in the sense in which we have used the term so far, atypical, although in approximately half of all adoptions one of the parents, usually the mother, is the natural parent of the child, or else the child is adopted by a relative (Wedge, 1973). In general, adoption appears to have achieved satisfactory results in terms of the children's educational attainment and adjustment, where representative samples have been investigated. For example, Seglow et al. (1972) compared the development of illegitimate adopted children from a large British cohort with their 'normal' contemporaries and found that their educational progress and behaviour compared favourably. In contrast, as we have seen above, illegitimate children remaining in one-parent families tend to be disadvantaged. Tizard's (1977) account of the follow-up of a small group of adopted children also gives a generally hopeful picture.

Children of working mothers can hardly now be said to be atypical since by secondary school age in Britain more than half of the child population have a working mother (most of whom, however, work part-time). At earlier ages, though, working mothers are still a minority, e.g. 20 per cent of children under five (OPCS, 1975). The evidence for any adverse effects on their children is slender (Ferri, 1976). Furthermore, there is some evidence that working-class children, especially boys, whose mothers work have higher educational attainments than those whose mothers do not, although for middle-class children the position may be reversed (Pugh, 1976). The important factors may be whether the working situation is seen in a positive light by the mother and whether the substitute care for the child, especially in the early years, is satisfactory.

Children from families who move frequently are often felt by teachers to be at a disadvantage because of the educational discontinuity and the severing of social contacts. However, it is difficult to establish firm evidence for this assessment since families who move home frequently are more likely to be one-parent families or to be

ocially mobile – in either direction. Whalen and Fried (1973) found
that mobile and less able children from lower socio-economic groups
tended to have lower educational attainment than their peers who
were not mobile. Ouston (1974), summarizing the rather scant
evidence, suggests that 'moving stimulates the child who is already
coping well at school, but may be too stressful for the less able child'.

Socially disadvantaged children

One further group of children who might be described as atypical
are those to whom the terms 'socially disadvantaged', 'culturally
disadvantaged', 'culturally deprived' or 'educationally disadvantaged' are frequently applied. As has been indicated earlier, this is
a controversial area of discussion. There is no doubt that children
from low income families, where the level of formal education and
the occupational skill of the parents is low, particularly where the
families are in poor housing, tend to make relatively poor educational
progress. Furthermore, their behaviour and adjustment are seen as
less satisfactory by their teachers than that of their peers from more
advantaged backgrounds. The controversy tends to centre upon
whether such children are appropriately seen as culturally deprived
by their home backgrounds or whether they come from sub-cultures
which are merely different from (rather than inferior to) that of the
prevailing and dominant culture in our society, which tends to
permeate schools' norms and values.

The extent of the educational disadvantage of such children in
Britain has been dramatically described and portrayed by Wedge and
Prosser (1973). Of their disadvantaged group, which comprised seven-
year-old children from large, low-income, poorly housed families, one
in six was receiving special help for educational backwardness compared with one in sixteen of a reference group of children with none
of these family circumstances. Only 7 per cent of the disadvantaged
were good readers compared with 38 per cent of the reference group.
They were similarly disadvantaged in maths; and one in four of the
disadvantaged group was judged to be 'maladjusted' in school whilst
only one in eleven of the more advantaged group fell into this category.
It is important to note, however, that the differences between the
groups ranged over a wide field of developmental and other difficulties. These included poor hearing and speech, ill-health, shorter
stature and more accidents in the home. Furthermore, the dis-

advantaged group were less likely to have been immunized against serious diseases and in general made less call upon preventive health services.

The main criticisms of the concept of cultural deprivation or disadvantage are that it devalues and denigrates working-class culture, it labels children and may therefore activate a self-fulfilling prophecy, and it distracts attention from the inequalities of an educational system which seeks to impose its middle-class values upon children and thus alienates working-class children and families. Much to his discomfiture, Bernstein was attacked by Labov (1970) for his views on the relationship between elaborated and restricted codes and social class. Bernstein demonstrated, according to Labov, 'a strong bias against all forms of working-class behaviour so that middle-class language is seen as superior in every respect'. Bernstein (1973) reacted sharply to this criticism and cited quotations from his earlier writings e.g. 'Clearly one code is not better than another, each possesses its own aesthetic, its own possibilities'; '... the notion of deficit is inadequate and perhaps misleading'. Bernstein concluded: 'These (deficit) theories offer little purchase upon the wide institutional and cultural contexts which define the form, content and evaluation of what is to be learned, how it is to be learned, and the organizational context'. Bernstein (1970) and Wilkerson (1970) in similar vein have criticized the concept of 'compensatory education' for stressing the inadequacies of children instead of focusing attention upon the inadequacies of schools.

Musgrove (1963) and Cronbach (1969) had earlier explicitly espoused the deficit view. For example, Musgrove's 'only regret' was that schools have largely failed in their task of 'cultural transformation' and of 'eradicating values and attitudes, habits and inclinations which may have 'an antique picturesqueness' but which are 'a serious liability' to a young person making his way in the world and trying to cast off the shackles of the 'backstreets in which he was reared'. Chazan (1973), in a more balanced treatment of this difficult issue concluded that 'the preservation of cultural differences is not incompatible with the achievement of equality of educational opportunity'; and Entwistle (1978) has more recently subjected this topic to a rigorous analysis.

Programmes of early intervention

The quickening of interest, particularly in the early 1960s in the US, in the possibility of early stimulation of children in order to accelerate cognitive growth was fostered by studies of pre-school intervention by, for example, Kirk (1958) and Weikart et al. (1964) and by influential analyses and commentaries by Hunt (1961) and Bloom (1964). This led to what is perhaps the best known and most extensive programme of early intervention, which was commenced in 1965, aimed largely at poor children and called 'Head Start'. This was later extended to include home-based intervention ('Home Start') and a follow-through into the public school system ('Follow-Through') (Karnes, 1969; Stanford Research Institute, 1971a and 1971b). However, the size of the programmes and the speed with which they were mounted – notably Head Start – meant that many of the individual programmes as well as the evaluations were ill-considered and firm conclusions have been difficult to draw.

One of the earliest and still one of the best known attempts to evaluate Head Start was carried out by the Westinghouse Learning Corporation (Cicirelli et al., 1969). They concluded that Head Start had had little effect on children's cognitive growth, as measured by IQ scores. Although others (e.g. Kagan, 1969; Hunt, 1969) were unconvinced by the Westinghouse and other analyses, a number of influential psychologists in the US concluded that Head Start and other intervention programmes were unsuccessful. For example, Jensen's (1969) widely quoted paper began with the sentence: 'Compensatory education has been tried and it apparently has failed'. Five years later Bronfenbrenner (1974a), commenting upon many of the attempts at early intervention until that time, stated: 'Although there were some modest achievements, by and large the results were disappointing. They were at best short-lived and small in magnitude.'

Nevertheless, Bronfenbrenner's (1974b) review of a relatively small number of well controlled and comparable longitudinal evaluations of pre-school programmes gave him more cause for optimism. Despite the 'tentative nature of the conclusions', he went on to postulate a number of significant general principles, which he has since developed in the context of an ecological model (1975 and 1977). Perhaps his most important conclusion was that 'for children from the most deprived groups no strategy of intervention is likely to be effective that focusses attention solely on the child or on the parent-child

relationship.... What is called for is intervention at the ecological
level, measures that will effect radical changes in the immediate
environment of the family and the child'.

Another, more recent examination in the US of a small number of
longitudinal studies of early intervention, which were 'carefully con
ceived and implemented with research designs and evaluation procedures from which conclusions can be drawn reliably' has concluded
that scholastic performance in the elementary grades can be improved
(Palmer, 1977). Palmer also makes a plea for a widening of the social
base of intervention programmes so that the many middle-class
children with special needs may be included.

The middle and later years of the 1970s saw further re-analyses
of the original Westinghouse data (e.g. Rinkskopf, 1976; Magidson,
1977) and yet more reviews of reports and studies. Brown (1977)
after one such review concludes about early intervention: 'We no
longer ask, "Does it work?" Now we ask: "How does it work?"
"For whom does it work?" and "How can it work better?"'

One of the most disappointing aspects of the American attempts
at evaluating programmes of early intervention has been the almost
universal acceptance of cognitive growth as the only significant objective. In many studies measured IQ is the overriding if not the only
yardstick of success or failure. One notable exception to this general
trend is Zigler (1973). He stresses the importance of motivation and
other factors. It would be of very little value, for example, to raise
the IQ level of poor Negroes if significant numbers continued to drop
out of education prematurely.

In Britain the most important document on early childhood education in the 1960s was the 'Plowden Report', a government enquiry
into primary schooling (Plowden, 1967). In addition to the research
which it sponsored and published on the relationship between home
environment and attainment, some of which we have already discussed, the Plowden Committee stimulated thinking and some action
on 'educational priority areas'. It was also largely responsible for the
small number of experiments and studies in early intervention which
started a few years later and which have continued in a rather low
key through the 1970s (e.g., Halsey, 1972; Midwinter, 1974; Poulton
and James, 1975; Van der Eyken and Shinman, 1977). The planned
expansion in nursery provision (DES, 1972), if it had not been
virtually stillborn, would no doubt have created and sustained much
more study and interest in this field.

The relative importance of home and school influences

We have already briefly considered some aspects of this topic in other contexts. The weight of research evidence has seemed to indicate that home environment is much more important than schooling in determining educational progress (e.g. Coleman, 1966; Peaker, 1967; Wiseman, 1967). We have also explored some of the difficulties of reaching any definitive conclusions about this (Goldstein, 1972; 1976). A point not referred to earlier but which poses another fundamental problem in interpreting the results of regression analysis is that the variation between home environments on almost any relevant measure which one could conceive is likely to be greater than the variation between school environments. This virtually prejudges their relative effects upon outcome measures of children's attainment.

However, in the 1970s in Britain there has been a small but growing body of research evidence that 'schools do make a difference' (e.g., Reynolds, 1976; 1977; 1978). Much of this work was stimulated by research by Power and his colleagues (1967; 1972), who carried out an interesting analysis of juvenile delinquency in a London borough. After examining a number of social and demographic variables, they concluded that the incidence of juvenile delinquency was associated in some measure with schools within the area. Unfortunately, the researchers were prevented from taking their work further. However, Reynolds has been able to pursue rather similar work at more depth in South Wales. Looking at nine secondary schools in a homogeneous, industrialized valley area, Reynolds has found wide and consistent differences between the schools over a number of years in school attendance, academic attainment and delinquency. These differences cannot, it seems, be explained in terms of catchment area, school intake, etc.

Gath (1972) and Rutter (1973) working in London boroughs, albeit with more superficial data, reached rather similar conclusions in terms of children's behaviour (Rutter) and of child guidance referral and delinquency (Gath).

These results have already prompted further work by Rutter in London and Reynolds in South Wales and, more recently, projects have been started on disaffection in a group of London schools by Kogan (1978) and on behaviour problems and learning difficulties in schools in Cardiff by Davie (1978). It is to be hoped that this body of research will throw further light upon the constructive role which schools can play in promoting mental health, satisfactory adjustment and good educational achievements and in combating alienation, underfunctioning and anti-social behaviour.

However, it has to be recognized that the dimensions of these and related problems are wide and complex and reach beyond the educational system. They extend into health care and the utilization of services; they have to do with standards of nutrition, with employment prospects, even with transport and other facilities in some areas. Schools have an important part to play which will necessitate difficult re-thinking and re-adjustment for them but the burden cannot be carried by schools alone. Unless the dimensions of the solution come nearer to matching the dimensions of the problem than they are at present, success is likely to be only partial.

References

Banks, O. and Finlayson, D. (1973) *Success and Failure in the Secondary School: An Interdisciplinary Approach to the School Achievement*. London: Methuen.

Bernstein, B. (1959) A public language: some sociological implications of linguistic form. *British Journal of Sociology 10*: 311–26.

Bernstein, B. (1960) Language and social class. *British Journal of Sociology 10*: 271–6.

Bernstein, B. (1970) Education cannot compensate for society. *New Society*, 26 February, 344–7.

Bernstein, B. (1973) A brief account of the theory of codes. In V. Lee (ed.) *Social Relationships and Language*. Bletchley: Open University Press.

Bloom, B. S. (1964) *Stability and Change in Human Characteristics*. New York: John Wiley.

Bronfenbrenner, U. (1974a) *Experimental Human Ecology: A Re-Orientation to Theory and Research on Socialization*.

Bronfenbrenner, U. (1974b) *Is Early Intervention Effective?* Washington, D.C.: US Dept of Health, Education and Welfare.

Bronfenbrenner, U. (1975) Reality and research in the ecology of human development. *Proceedings of the American Philosophical Society 119* (6): 439–69.

Bronfenbrenner, U. (1977) *The Experimental Ecology of Human Development*. Harvard: Harvard University Press.

Brown, B. (1977) *Long-term Gains from Early Intervention: An Overview of Current Research*. Paper presented to American Association for the Advancement of Science, Denver.

Chazan, M. (1973) The concept of compensatory education. In M. Chazan (ed.) *Compensatory Education*. London: Butterworth.

Cicirelli, V. G., Granger, R. L. et al. (1969) *The Impact of Headstart*. Report to the US Office of Economic Opportunity by Westinghouse Learning Corporation and Ohio University

Coleman, J. S. et al. (1966) *Equality of Educational Opportunity*. Washington, D.C.: US Office of Education.

Cronbach, L. (1969) Heredity, environment and educational policy. *Harvard Educational Review 39*: 338–47.

Davie, R. (1973) Eleven years of childhood. *Statistical News*, August: 14–18.

Davie, R. (1978) Evaluation and monitoring of the effectiveness of a university based course on behaviour and learning problems in schools. Unpublished paper, University College, Cardiff.

Davie, R., Butler, N. and Goldstein, H. (1972) *From Birth to Seven*. London: Longman.

Department of Education and Science (1972) *Education: A Framework for Expansion*. London: HMSO.

Douglas, J. W. B. (1967) *The Home and the School*. London: Panther Books.

Douglas, J. W. B., Ross, J. and Simpson, H. R. (1968) *All Our Future*. London: Peter Davies.

Douglas, J. W. B. (1970) Broken families and child behaviour. *Journal of the Royal College of Physicians 4* (3): 203–10.

Entwistle, H. (1978) *Class, Culture and Education*. London: Methuen.

Ferri, E. (1976) *Growing Up in a One-Parent Family*. Windsor: National Foundation for Educational Research.

Floud, J. (1962). The sociology of education. In T. D. Welford et al. (eds) *Society: Problems and Methods of Study*. London: Routledge and Kegan Paul.

Floud, J. E., Halsey, A. H. and Martin, F. M. (1956) *Social Class and Educational Opportunity*. London: Heinemann.

Fogelman, K. R. and Goldstein, H. (1976) Social factors associated with changes in educational attainment between 7 and 11. *Educational Studies*, June.

Fraser, E. (1959) *Home Environment and the School*. London: University of London Press.

Gath, D. (1972) Child guidance and delinquency in a London borough. *Psychological Medicine 2*: 185–91.

George, V. and Wilding, P. (1972) *Motherless Families*. London: Routledge and Kegan Paul.

Ginsburg, H. (1972) *The Myth of the Deprived Child*. Englewood Cliffs: Prentice Hall.

Goldstein, H. (1972) Home and school – Plowden re-examined. *Times Educational Supplement* 5.5.72.

Goldstein, H. (1976) Whose values in educational research? *Bias 3* (1): 1–7.

Halsey, A. H. (ed.) (1972) *Educational Priority*, Vol. 1. London: HMSO.

Havighurst, R. (1971) Social class and human development. In F. J. Mönks, Willard W. Hartup and Jan de Wit (eds) *Determinants of Behavioural Development*. New York and London: Academic Press.

Hunt, J. McV. (1961) *Intelligence and Experience*. New York: Ronald Press.

Hunt, J. McV. (1969) Has compensatory education failed? Has it been attempted? *Harvard Educational Review 39* (2): 278–300.

Jackson, B. and Marsden, D. (1962) *Education and the Working Class*. London: Routledge and Kegan Paul.

142   The School Years

Jensen, A. R. (1969) How much can we boost IQ and scholastic achievement? *Harvard Educational Review* 39 (1): 1–123.

Kagan, J. S. (1969) Inadequate evidence and illogical conclusions. *Harvard Educational Review* 39 (2): 274–7.

Karnes, M. B. (1969) *Research and Development Program on Pre-school Disadvantaged Children*. Washington, D.C.: US Office of Education.

Kirk, S. A. (1958) *Early Education of the Mentally Retarded*. Urbana, Illinois: University of Illinois Press.

Kogan, M. (1978) Study of problem pupils in Outer London secondary schools – disaffected pupils project. List 1, Current Educational Research Projects Supported by the Dept of Education and Science. London: DES.

Labov, W. (1970) The logic of nonstandard English. In F. Williams (ed.) *Language and Poverty*. New York: Markham Press.

Magidson, J. (1977) *Towards a Causal Model Approach for Adjusting for Pre-existing Differences in the Non-equivalent Control Group Situation: A General Alternative to ANCOVA*. Cambridge, Mass.: Abt. Associates.

Midwinter, E. (ed.) (1974) *Preschool Priorities*. London: Ward Lock Educational.

Musgrove, F. (1963) *The Migratory Elite*. London: Heinemann.

OPCS (1975) *Census 1971. England and Wales: Household Composition Tables.* Table 53. London: HMSO.

Ouston, J. (1974) Children from families who move frequently. *Highlight No. 10*. London: National Children's Bureau.

Palmer, F. H. (1977) The effects of early childhood educational intervention on school performance. Unpublished paper, State University of New York.

Peaker, G. F. (1967) The regression analyses of the national survey. Appendix 4, Vol. 2 *Children and Their Primary Schools*. London: HMSO.

Plowden, Lady (Chmn) (1967) *Children and Their Primary Schools*. 2 vols. London: HMSO.

Poulton, G. A. and James, T. (1975) *Pre-School Learning in the Community: Strategies for Change*. London and Boston: Routledge and Kegan Paul.

Power, M. J. et al. (1967) Delinquent schools. *New Society*, 19 October.

Power, M. J. et al. (1972) Neighbourhood, school and juveniles before the courts. *British Journal of Criminology* 12: 111–32.

Pringle, M. K., Butler, N. R. and Davie, R. (1966) *11,000 Seven-Year-Olds*. London: Longman.

Pugh, G. (1976) Children of working mothers. *Highlight No. 22*. London: National Children's Bureau.

Reynolds, D. (1976) Schools do make a difference. *New Society*, 29 July.

Reynolds, D. (1977) The delinquent school. In H. Hammersley and P. Woods (eds) *The Process of Schooling*. London: Routledge and Kegan Paul.

Reynolds, D. (1978) Education and the prevention of juvenile delinquency. In N. S. Tutt (ed.) *Alternative Strategies for Coping with Crime*. London: Basil Blackwell.

Rinkskopf, D. (1976) *A Comparison of Various Regression-Correction Methods for Evaluating Non-experimental Research*. Doctoral dissertation, Iowa State University.

Rutter, M. (1971) Parent–child separation. *Journal of Child Psychology and Psychiatry 12* (4): 233–60.

Rutter, M. (1973) Why are London children so disturbed? *Proceedings of the Royal Society 66*: 121–5.

Rutter, M. (1975) *Helping Troubled Children.* London: Penguin Books.

Seglow, J., Pringle, M. K. and Wedge, P. (1972) *Growing Up Adopted.* Windsor: National Foundation for Educational Research.

Stanford Research Institute (1971a) *Preliminary Evaluation of Planned Variation in Head Start According to Follow-Through Approaches (1969–70).* Washington, D.C.: OCD, US Dept of Health, Education and Welfare.

Stanford Research Institute (1971b) *Longitudinal Evaluation of Selected Features of the National Follow-Through Program.* Washington, D.C.: OCD, US Dept of Health, Education and Welfare.

Tizard, B. (1977) *Adoption: A Second Chance.* London: Open Books.

Van Der Eyken, W. and Shinman, S. (1977) Report on SSRC-supported pre-school research project. Unpublished paper, London: Social Science Research Council.

Wedge, P. and Prosser, H. (1973) *Born to Fail?* London: Arrow Books.

Wedge, P. (1973) On the adoption horizon. *Child Adoption 73* (3): 28–34.

Weikart, D. P., Kamii, C. K. and Radin, N. (1964) *Perry Pre-School Progress Report.* Ypsilanti, Michigan: Ypsilanti Public Schools.

Whalen, T. E. and Fried, M. A. (1973) Geographical mobility and its effect on student achievement. *Journal of Educational Research 67* (4):

Wilkerson, D. A. (1970) Compensatory programs across the nation. In A. H. Passow (ed.) *Reaching the Disadvantaged Learner.* New York: Teachers College Press.

Wiseman, S. (1967) The Manchester Survey. Appendix 9, Vol. 2 *Children and their Primary Schools.* London: HMSO.

Wiseman, S. (1972) Education and environment. In M. Craft et al. (eds) *Linking Home and School* (2nd edition). London: Longman.

Zigler, E. F. (1970) Social class and the socialization process. *Review of Educational Research 40* (1): 87–110.

Zigler, E. F. (1973) Project Head Start: success or failure? *Children Today 2*: 2–7.

7 Juvenile delinquency

Rodney Maliphant

There is probably no other social problem that has attracted so much attention from so many persons of such diverse disciplines as delinquency. In recent times it has been the subject of particular concern to central government both in this country (HMSO, 1963; 1965; 1968a and b; 1969) and in the United States (US Government, 1967; 1974). This is not surprising in view of the increasing size of the problem. It has been estimated that between 10 and 20 per cent of the male population can be expected to have had at least one conviction for a criminal offence by the time they reach the age of eighteen (Hood and Sparks, 1970). In city areas of course, the proportion would be higher. West and Farrington (1977) report that 30·8 per cent of the London boys, whom they first interviewed at age eight, had been convicted by the time the majority of them had reached twenty-one (24·9 per cent by age eighteen).

Sociologists, psychiatrists and psychologists over decades have produced many ideas about the cause, treatment and, less frequently, the prevention of delinquency. Such terms in themselves, of course, imply notions about the nature of delinquency and how it may be explained. These will be considered later although a comprehensive review of recent developments in sociological theory (Taylor et al., 1973) will not be possible.

Space also prevents any detailed consideration of delinquency in girls. Surprisingly, it has not attracted much research interest until recently (Cowie et al., 1968; Goodman, 1976; Campbell, 1977), presumably because of its relatively low incidence.

Emphasis will be given to findings reported in the United Kingdom. First, general problems in defining delinquency and determining incidence will be considered.

Problems of definition

There would seem to be no difficulty in identifying juvenile delinquents. Delinquents are those young persons (aged 10 to 17 in England and Wales) who have been convicted by the courts (for Scotland see HMSO, 1968b). Unfortunately, for many reasons, defining who is delinquent and assessing the incidence of delinquency is by no means as simple as might be supposed.

First, there is the obvious point: not all who are delinquent are detected, not all who are detected are reported, not all who are reported appear before the courts – and not all those who do so are convicted. Furthermore, Radzinowicz (1964) suggests that only about 15 per cent of all crimes committed in England are officially recorded; Jones (1965) gives an estimate of 25 per cent. It is likely that very serious crimes, particularly those involving considerable theft, are more accurately recorded, since such losses have to be made good. However, other crimes which might prove embarrassing to the victim if made public (e.g. sexual assault or fraud perpetrated within the family) are more likely to be grossly under-represented.

Two strategies have usually been adopted in an attempt to arrive at a more accurate notion of incidence: the use of self-report studies and interviews with victims. Hood and Sparks (1970) comment on both.

There are two main drawbacks to self-report studies published so far. No investigator has yet taken a representative sample of young people from a specific area for which there are comparable crime statistics and confined enquiries from respondents to a specific time period. Belson (1975), using data from interviews with 1,425 London boys, found that they all admitted to some stealing at some time in their lives. Such admissions were spread across all socio-economic groups but with some slight increase amongst working-class boys; 13 per cent of the boys claimed they had been caught by the police at some time (these appeared to have been more heavily involved in stealing than others). Other research has usually confirmed that social class differences are less marked when self-report data are used. Nevertheless, those who admit to more delinquency also tended to be more frequently known to the police, with boys from lower socio-economic groups being over-represented (e.g. Douglas et al., 1966; Gold, 1966; McDonald, 1969; West and Farrington, 1977). A second general problem with all self-report studies is the difficulty in establishing the validity of the admissions made. Not only is the investigator dependent on the memory of the young person but there is also the difficulty in deciding whether the description of the delinquent behaviour has been deliberately limited or over-elaborated. Christie (1968) concluded that self-report studies regrettably have limitations just as official records have: 'We have exchanged the official system of registration for some social scientist's system of registration.' Christie et al. (1965), from their study of self-reported crime, also make the further statement, now fairly widely supported: 'The official system does not select its cases at random. By and large it is the case that the small group of officially registered criminals have also been involved in the largest amount of crime.' This appears to apply to both children and adults.

The second main strategy adopted to clarify how accurately official crime figures reflect actual incidence has been to use interviews with victims. By definition, of course, such a technique can give no data on offences where there has been no victim or where the victim cannot be identified. Hood and Sparks (1970) indicate that within these confines such a technique has produced a good match with official records when serious crimes have been involved. However, petty offences tended to be under-represented, presumably because the victim did not think them worth mentioning or had forgotten them. This also applied to the householder's recall of offences against other members of the household not interviewed.

Other more formal limitations of official crime statistics relate to changes in legislation, court and police practice. For example, in England and Wales, the minimal age of criminal responsibility (permitting criminal proceedings to be taken) was raised from eight to ten years of age in 1964. The 1969 Children's Act (HMSO, 1969) made provision to raise it ultimately to age fourteen as well as to restrict the use of committals to penal institutions. However, these provisions so far have not been fully implemented. This Act coupled with the development of police liaison bureaux schemes (which existed

before the 1969 Act), the use of day attendance centres, and cautioning procedures, have induced marked changes in dealing with children
in trouble.

The principal aims of the 1969 Act were to reduce the number
of children appearing before the courts and to provide a more
comprehensive and flexible system of treatment with increased provision within the community (Ford, 1975). The problem of dealing
with children in trouble has received similar consideration in Scotland
(HMSO, 1968b). It is too early to assess the efficacy of such changes
but the new Scottish system appears to have avoided to some extent
the confusion and conflict between judicial and disposition functions
(Taylor et al., 1976). In England and Wales, the juvenile courts may
now make two main kinds of court orders – supervision and care
orders. Supervision orders can be made of up to three years duration,
with the facility of attached conditions (under Section 12) for treatment within the community if needed. This is termed 'intermediate
treatment' and may utilize not only the established services provided
by the local authority but also the initiatives and interests of voluntary
organizations and private persons within the community. The social
services department of the local authority or the probation service
are responsible for the actual supervision. The second form of order
is the care order which can be of much longer duration for it places
the local authority in loco parentis with placement and 'treatment'
determined by its social services department. This might result in the
child being placed in a community home (to 1973 named 'children's
home', with 'approved schools' for delinquents) or with foster parents
or indeed in his own home. However, before such an order can be
made, the court must be satisfied that it is essential to secure the child's
welfare and proper development; the normal rules of evidence in court
also still apply. It will be clear that with the court's lack of direct
control over disposition or treatment, there is an implicit and pressing
need to maintain the highest level of communication between all
agencies, the police, the courts, the education and medical services
and the social services department, if mutual confidence in each
other's functions is to be maintained. Regional planning committees
have been set up to encourage the development of facilities by local
authorities, who may submit schemes for approval to the central
government's Department of Health and Social Security. However,
these regional planning committees have no statutory powers to
impose changes at the local authority level.

The working of the Act has been affected by a number of general factors which probably contribute to the many criticisms made. In 1970, through the Local Authority Social Services Act (HMSO, 1970; HMSO 1968c) most welfare services for all sections and ages in the community were integrated into one department, the social services department, responsible to the central government's Department of Health and Social Security. Previously, as the Children's Department, it had been concerned only with children and young persons in need of care or protection and was responsible to the Home Office. As such, its staff had progressively developed their own skills in dealing with children and family breakdowns. The local authority's probation services were also much more heavily involved in the specialized work of supervising and counselling juvenile delinquents than they are now.

The massive integration of several professionally skilled groups into one department dealing with a wide spectrum of problems and age groups (plus a change in central government control) was immediately followed by a further Act, the Local Government Act (HMSO, 1972), which involved major changes in local government boundaries, the trend being towards creating larger local authorities. Further problems relating to the integration of services were inevitable (Ford, 1975).

The working of the 1969 Children and Young Persons Act has recently been considered by a Government Committee (HMSO, 1975a). The Act has been criticized on many grounds, such as:

(1) It blurs over the distinctive functions of police, court and local authority in relation to the welfare of children, the establishment of guilt and the safeguarding of the public interest. It confuses punishment and treatment without advantage to the young offender, parent or the community.

(2) The resources of departments of social services are inadequate, in terms of both staffing and expertise, to meet the multiplicity of problems with which they are now confronted.

(3) The expected increase in the use of community based measures has not been as great as expected. In fact there has been increased use of custodial measures (Taylor et al., 1976; HMSO, 1977a). This could reflect the difficulties facing local services in containing particularly difficult children in the accommodation they have available. Community home staff may refuse to take such children if they feel they cannot

integrate them with other children already resident. The increased use of custodial measures could also reflect a lack of
confidence by the police and the courts in alternative provision. It is worthy of note that since August 1977 the Home
Secretary has imposed more stringent criteria to limit the
number of juveniles remanded to prison, under Section 69 of
the 1975 Children Act (HMSO, 1975b).

Concern over the effectiveness of intervention procedures and programmes, both for delinquents and others, of course existed long before
the implementation of the 1969 Children's Act.

In initiating prosecutions the police obviously make use of their
discretionary powers (Hood and Sparks, 1970). An informal caution
may be used for a relatively minor offence as part of the police juvenile
liaison scheme. While the seriousness of the offence and the strength
of the evidence will be the main determinants of police action, know-
edge of the boy and his family background will also contribute to
the decision to take matters further. In general, relatively fewer
children from lower socio-economic backgrounds are likely to be dealt
with informally, presumably because the police, from their experience,
consider such children as less likely to modify their behaviour
as a result of parental action and neighbourhood influences. Such
factors, together with variations in practice between police forces
e.g. in the use of formal cautioning (HMSO, 1977a)) will influence
the nature and volume of delinquency which is finally recorded but
it is impossible to say to what degree.

Further difficulties arise even after a person has been found guilty
of an offence. These will now be considered.

Offences: incidence and type

Official criminal statistics in England and Wales are usually broadly
classified into two groups – non-indictable and indictable, approxi-
mating to the less serious and serious offences respectively.

31·1 per cent of males and 20·1 per cent of females under seventeen years of age, convicted in 1976, had committed non-indictable
offences (based on HMSO, 1977a). Girls accounted for only 6·8 per
cent of all such offences in this age group. About half of the boys and
a quarter of the girls had convictions for motoring offences.

The majority of convictions in this under-seventeen age group
relate to the more serious (indictable) offences and these are com-

mitted mostly by boys. Girls accounted for only 10·9 per cent of suc[h]
offences although this rises to 16·9 per cent if formal cautioning i[s]
included (see HMSO, 1977a, p. 31). Cautioning tends to be use[d]
more frequently with girls and with both sexes if under the age o[f]
fourteen or fifteen. However, there are huge differences across th[e]
country in terms of police practice. For example, 25 per cent of a[ll]
males under seventeen found guilty or cautioned for indictabl[e]
offences (HMSO, 1977) were cautioned in Cleveland but in Wiltshir[e]
the percentage was 67!

Indictable offences are subdivided into eight classes: violenc[e]
against the person, sexual offences, burglary, robbery, theft an[d]
handling stolen goods, fraud and forgery, criminal damage an[d]
miscellaneous. The table indicates the distribution of convictions wit[h]
cautionings, by type and sex, for the under-seventeen age group. Th[e]
preponderance of theft and associated activities is very marked an[d]

Table 7.1   Young persons under the age of seventeen found guilty or
cautioned for indictable offences, England and Wales, 1976 (Based on
HMSO, 1977a, p. 37)

	Males		Females	
	N	*Per cent*	*N*	*Per cent*
Violence against the person	4,434	4·5	1,426	4.8
Sexual offences	2,189	1·5 ⎫	30	0·1 ⎫
Burglary	38,041	26·4 ⎪ 82·5	1,964	6·7 ⎪ 89·4
Robbery	1,054	0·7 ⎪	111	0·4 ⎪
Theft and handling stolen goods	79,965	55·4 ⎭	24,179	82·3 ⎭
Fraud and forgery	1,261	0·9	527	1·8
Criminal damage	14,971	10·4	1,053	3·6
Other offences	323	0·2	82	0·3
Total convictions/ cautionings for indictable offences	144,238	100·0	29,327	100·0
Percentage of all convictions in age group 10 to 17		83·1		16·9
Percentage of all convictions (indictable offences) – all ages for each sex		34·1		32·5

particularly so for girls. This may reflect increased prosecutions for shoplifting. It will also be noted that this school age group, from ten to seventeen, contributed about a third of all indictable convictions for all ages for each sex.

A slight fall in indictable offences in relation to the population age group at risk has been maintained over the years 1975 and 1976. The peak age for convictions and formal cautioning for indictable offences was fifteen for boys and fourteen for girls in 1976.

These figures of course relate to offences that have been 'cleared up' by the police as a result of a finding of guilt or a formal caution. However, not all offences recorded by the police are 'cleared up'. The 'cleared up' rate for indictable offences over the last five years has ranged from 43 to 46 per cent but this is an 'average' figure (HMSO, 1977a, p. 29). The highest cleared-up rates for specific groups of offences in 1976 were 81 per cent for fraud and forgery and 79 per cent for violence against the person (with 93 per cent for the miscellaneous group). Table 7.1 indicates that none of these types of offences were numerically very large in relation to the total number of convictions for indictable offences. In contrast, the lowest cleared-up rates were for robbery (34 per cent), criminal damage (35 per cent) and theft and handling stolen goods (41 per cent). Thus, although convictions for theft and handling stolen goods are the most numerous there are also many more known to the police which have not resulted in a conviction. If these are combined with other activities related to theft, such as burglary and robbery, it will be seen how ignorant we are about who commits the numerically largest categories of indictable crime (theft and burglary). If the estimates of crimes *not* recorded by the police are at all accurate, (85 per cent estimate – Radzinowicz, 1964; 75 per cent – Jones, 1965) are combined with the low 'cleared up' rates for known crimes, our lack of knowledge about who commits crime, particularly theft, appears huge, even on the basis of official statistics.

Classifying delinquents by the offence for which they have been convicted has not proved very profitable (Gibbons, 1965) for few criminals or juvenile delinquents habitually commit similar offences. Even if delinquents had homogeneous records of offences, the psychological value of such a classification would still have limited value. Since the majority of crimes involve theft (see Table 7.1), a system using classification by offence only would not have much discriminating power. Furthermore, offences of theft and others will vary in extent, criminal sophistication and motivation, (e.g. from stealing a bar of chocolate when hungry to a planned entry into a warehouse just for monetary gain). A crime of violence can range from a minor injury resulting from a door being slammed in a shopkeeper's face as a boy escapes with a packet of sweets, to an unprovoked assault on an elderly person. Thus the same offence may encompass a highly varied range of behaviour. Similar offences may have different motivational sources and different offences may share similar sources. Inferences drawn from type of offence can therefore easily be misleading. Thus a young offender may have been convicted for the relatively minor offence of taking and driving away a motor vehicle without the owner's consent, but the actual taking of the car could have been part of a deliberate and highly sophisticated piece of criminal planning in which transport formed an essential part. The psychological value of formal offence description is thus minimal since identical crimes in law may still be highly varied in behaviour and motivation. Research which combines knowledge of the offender with a detailed analysis of situational factors relating to the offence appears non-existent, presumably because of the methodological difficulties presented. Retrospective accounts by the offender have obvious limitations although consensus in reports by witnesses and victims at least for some offences, could prove helpful if given in sufficient detail soon after the offence has been committed. For the time being there would appear to be only largely subjective but none the less valuable descriptive accounts that can link the person with the situation and possible conditions that elicit crime (e.g., Parker, 1974).

Recidivism

Delinquency has so far been considered in relation to type of offence and incidence only. The persistence of delinquency over time has yet to be considered. It has generally been found that about half of those convicted as first offenders do not offend again (Power et al., 1972; Rutter and Madge, 1976; West, 1967). The proportion is likely to vary both in relation to time at risk after the first conviction as well as the sample used. West and Farrington (1977) indicate that 39 out of their 101 London offenders (38·6 per cent) had no further convictions up to the age of eighteen or nineteen. In the United States Wolfgang et al. (1972) report that 56 per cent of their larger sample had no further convictions to age twenty-seven. If approximately 5 per cent of first offenders do not offend again perhaps they should not be considered real delinquents.

Many attempts have been made to measure the seriousness of delinquency (Sellin and Wolfgang, 1964). The limitations of type of offence as an index of actual behaviour have already been indicated. The sentence given for an offence provides a fairly crude but not un-contaminated measure of the court's judgement but such a measure would be even less appropriate for young persons in view of the current functions of the juvenile court resulting from the implementation of the 1969 Children's Act.

Much research has used reconviction counts as a measure of recidivism but such counts can be distorted by unspecified variations in the time at risk. For example, delinquents placed in institutions are not usually at liberty to commit further offences whereas a person who is fined or on probation can do so. So far, it has not been possible to identify those who will become delinquent or those who will persist in their delinquency, without including far too many 'false-positives' or incorrect choices (Simon, 1971). A high degree of accuracy has been claimed for the Glueck Social Prediction Scale (Glueck and Glueck, 1960). However, this scale has been subject to much criticism primarily because it is based on an 'artificial' sample in which 50 per cent were delinquent (Banks, 1964; Walters, 1956; Hirschi and Selvin, 1967). Wilkins (1969) also observes: 'No prediction is proved by the same data that were used to establish it in the first place.... Where sound validation studies have been attempted, the power of the prediction has dropped markedly, especially in cases where the prediction was based on subjective assessments.'

Since approximately 50 per cent of delinquents do not offend again after their first court appearance, the real problem in delinquency must be the recidivist or 'repeater'. Follow-up data from the Cambridge Study (West and Farrington, 1977) suggests that not only are there real personal differences between delinquents and non-delinquents from the same area, but that teachers can identify future delinquents with some success much earlier in their school careers. How accurately they are able to do it without pulling in too many wrong choices, as often occurs in prediction scales, needs to be established in a further prospective study.

In view of the many difficulties in identifying delinquents and the nature of their delinquent behaviour, it is perhaps not surprising that research is still functioning at a fairly crude level of analysis with, still, regrettably little integration of the sociological and psychological approaches. Cynically, it might be asserted that both the social and personal characteristics of delinquents are determined by the selective actions of the police and the courts. Such a view savours of the 'Eden-ideology' coined by Walker (1977) – Adam and Eve in the Garden of Eden being 'happy and harmless nudists until they were "criminalized" by the knowledge of good and evil and the punishment of Jehovah'! Whatever the qualifications to official statistics, the fact that delinquents are the subject of public concern is sufficient justification for investigation (Tappan, 1947). Furthermore, as Wilkins (1969) says: '... what defines a society more efficiently than its failures? What better indication of the state of development of a people than the people it cannot integrate, accommodate or accept? What reveals the nature of a society's goals more clearly than the way it deals with those who fail to achieve them?'

Some consideration will now be given to the ecological, social and personal attributes of delinquents.

Social ecological approaches to delinquency

This term has been adopted for what are primarily studies of the spatial distribution of delinquency (Baldwin, 1975; Morris, 1957). Whether it is appropriate to use the concepts of plant ecology would appear to be doubtful, for human adaptation is complex and as much dependent on collaboration as it is upon competition. Furthermore, man does not just adapt to the environment, he also creates much of it (Maliphant, 1972).

There is likely to be little dispute about where the majority of delinquents live. Area studies in this country (e.g. Burt, 1925; Castle and Gittus, 1957; Morris, 1957; Wallis and Maliphant, 1967) and in the United States (e.g. Shaw and McKay, 1942; 1969; Lander, 1954; Schmid, 1960) are generally agreed in identifying high delinquency areas as urban environments where there is high industrial or commercial development, a decreasing population, lack of open-space recreation areas and poor housing, with overcrowding. Health indices, with the exception of mortality rates in recent years, tend to be less favourable, unemployment rates are high and relatively more young people are leaving school with minimal education. However, there would appear to be some differences between the attributes of high delinquency areas. Specific indices of 'social disorganization'

(Lander, 1954), such as suicide rates, divorce rates and mental illness, appear to correlate highly in the United States with delinquency rates as well as with the area attributes already mentioned. This was not found to be so in London (Wallis and Maliphant, 1967) although a study in Liverpool (Castle and Gittus, 1957) did indicate similar associations. No doubt the way cities have developed, as well as the population they attract, are relevant to such differences that are found. However, in general, the attributes of high delinquency areas appear remarkably consistent in both the United Kingdom and the United States. In spite of changes over time in the population of cities, re-housing schemes, the effects of bomb damage during the last war, and changes in the economic climate, the adverse attributes of delinquency areas relative to others have remained. The high delinquency areas also usually remain high whatever kind of delinquent sample is used (i.e. whether probationers or institutionalized delinquents; whether old or young). Shaw and McKay (1969) report highly significant correlations over some 30 years (0·61 to 0·85) in the same cities for delinquency rates based on samples varying in their criminal records. Using different age samples, the correlations with delinquency rates were also high, ranging from 0·79 to 0·90 for five American cities. In this country, Burt's (1925) delinquency rates for London, based on 2,000 boys and girls from reformatory schools, correlated significantly (0·54) with rates based on a small but representative sample of institutionalized young offenders aged sixteen to twenty from London, interviewed some 40 years after these data were collected (Wallis and Maliphant, 1967). The rates produced by Wallis and Maliphant also correlated significantly (0·70) with a younger school aged sample collected by Power (1966).

Such consistency over time, across different samples and different countries, requires rather more attention than just the recognition that most delinquents live in socially and economically depressed areas (Wootton, 1959). The implications are that such adverse environments either attract delinquency-prone persons or encourage, in some way, delinquent behaviour. It needs to be noted, of course, that the environment does indeed provide an excess of opportunities for delinquent enterprises, with its warehouses and business premises unoccupied except during working hours.

It is surprising that except for one isolated instance reported in Shaw and McKay (1969), no data are known to have been published where area recidivist rates are based on the original parent sample.

Thus although high delinquency rates remain high over time and variations in the criminality and age of the sample, there is little evidence to indicate whether such areas actually 'produce' a disproportionate number of recidivists. The one study, briefly reported by Shaw and McKay, gives correlations from 0·67 to 0·74 between delinquency rates and recidivist rates derived from the same sample. This would suggest that the attributes of delinquency areas are associated in some way not only with delinquency but with continuing delinquency. Maliphant (1972), using several indices of recidivism, correlated area delinquency rates with recidivist rates, based on a London sample of institutionalized young offenders at three points in time (representing approximately a ten year follow-up period). All correlations were near zero. Such findings need cautious interpretation since the sample was small, although considered to be representative in relation to national crime figures. It is also possible that the findings might be different with a younger aged sample who could be more reactive, in terms of behaviour, to conditions existing in socially depressed areas. The level of analysis in delinquency area research is of course extremely crude, with rates based on boroughs or census tracts (USA). Power et al. (1972) found less marked differences between areas within one London borough.

Although area attributes cannot be accorded to individuals (Robinson, 1950) it is necessary to try to discover how conditions of the environment are transmuted to effect the behaviour of individuals. The follow-up of a sample of institutionalized delinquents into adulthood by Glueck and Glueck (1969) did indicate that their delinquents at age 31 still usually occupied worse accommodation and experienced more difficulties than their matched, non-delinquent controls. Unfortunately, it is difficult to assess accurately what changes took place within and between the two groups over time as the sample contracted and variables were changed for the follow-up investigation. Stott (1960), using his own Bristol Social Adjustment Guide, carried out a limited exploration of the association of 'unfavourable ecology' to delinquency and maladjustment. His study indicated that unlike their non-delinquent peers, delinquents had similar scores for maladjustment even with increasingly 'unfavourable ecology'. Unfortunately, his measure of maladjustment is confined to the Social Adjustment Guide completed by teachers and he did not explore ecological differences in any detail.

The so-called ecological approach to delinquency has been one of the cornerstones for the development of sociological theory. However, the difficulty for psychologists is in determining why some individuals, but not others, should be influenced by the social and economic conditions to become delinquent. This need for a personal differentiating element is recognized by many sociologists. With Lander (1954) and others, Inkeles (1961) has asserted that 'the attempt to understand the structure and functioning of social systems will often require the use of a general theory of personality and knowledge of the distinctive personality characteristics of participants in the system' (p. 272). He criticizes Shaw and McKay's work on the grounds that they failed 'to specify the mechanisms by means of which a quality of the community could be translated into the individual actions which ultimately produce the delinquency rate'.

Peer group influences

Delinquents, as already indicated, tend to live in close proximity and in similar conditions in urban environments. Most of their crimes are also committed in the company of others. Not surprisingly, they also tend to have more delinquent friends than their non-delinquent peers (Glueck and Glueck, 1950). On these grounds alone, the importance of peer group influences in initiating, maintaining or indeed perhaps restraining delinquent behaviour are obviously important areas for investigation. Much of the research to date has been based on demonstrating associations but in themselves these cannot establish causes or the direction of effects. Although delinquents tend to have delinquent friends, for example, it is important to know whether such friendships existed before or after the initial delinquency (Hirschi and Selvin, 1967). Hirschi (1969), in reviewing the evidence, takes the view that 'the boy's stake in conformity affects his choice of friends rather than the other way round'.

It is sometimes suggested that peer group values are more likely to take precedence over others when there are unsatisfactory family relationships, as is often the case with delinquents. However, it would appear that delinquents generally have more unsatisfactory relationships at all levels, both within their own homes and with their peers. On commonsense grounds and the statements of boys who have stopped being delinquent (e.g. West and Farrington, 1977), the avoidance of delinquent friends would seem to be a factor in reform but the reasons for taking such a course need much more extensive investigation. The importance of juvenile gangs (defined as groups with a relatively constant membership and structure) would seem to be far less in this country than elsewhere, although clearly some do exist (O'Hagan, 1976).

The contribution of family factors and personality characteristics to delinquency will now be considered.

Family factors in delinquency

Burt (1925) claimed on his evidence that the child's relations with his parents were more important than other environmental influences, such as poverty, and that 'mental dullness' and 'temperamental instability, which is not abnormal enough to be considered pathological', were important personality characteristics of delinquents. Recent studies do much to confirm these early findings. West and Farrington (1977) report five background variables significantly related to delinquency in their sample of London working-class boys. These variables were low income, family size, poor parental behaviour, parental criminality and low intelligence of the boys. Over half of their recidivists came from poor homes. Since family size has always been highly related to social class groupings, its association with delinquency is not surprising. However, West (1977) suggests that the number of siblings competing for the parents' limited resources is probably the more relevant variable. The finding that delinquents often hold a medial position in their families should occasion no surprise since the probability that this will be so obviously increases with the size of the family. Glueck and Glueck (1950) also stressed the importance of the boy's relationship with the parents, particularly the mother, and the cohesiveness of the family.

The significance of broken homes and separation from parents, other than by death, has long been associated with delinquency. However, recent findings (Rutter, 1971; West and Farrington, 1973; Power et al., 1972) have confirmed a much earlier statement made by Shaw and McKay (1932) that 'The actual divorce or separation from parents may not be so important a factor in the life of the child as the emotional conflicts which have resulted in the break in family relationships'. Bowlby (1946) emphasized the importance of early mother–child separation in relation to the development of the delinquent 'affectionless character', although this emphasis was somewhat modified in a later paper (Bowlby et al., 1956). McCord et al.

(1959) also stressed the importance of parent–child relationships and how one parent could compensate for the inadequacies of the other. Andry (1960) provided a useful emphasis on the importance of the father in relation to delinquent behaviour in boys.

The processing of data on family relationships and delinquency has inevitably been reduced to an analysis of dyads, father–child and mother–child (with little on sibling relationships). Yet the quality of the relationship within each dyad is a part-function of all the other existing relationships within the family. Factors of age, the availability of acceptable parent-surrogates, the duration and intensity of discord must also contribute to the individual's reaction to stress in family relationships.

Personality characteristics

The average IQ for a group of delinquents is usually within the low average range, approximately IQ 90–95. However, the range of IQs is very wide, showing considerable overlap with the 'normal' population (Woodward, 1955; West and Farrington, 1973). Nevertheless West and Farrington, using a non-verbal test (Raven's Progressive Matrices), report that their London delinquents were generally less intelligent than their non-delinquent peers, and the recidivists were more so. They could find no evidence that the low test scores were due to poor attention or low motivation. Tennent and Gath (1975) report a small follow-up study of two groups of delinquents of above average and average intelligence but they found no differences in reconviction rates for the two groups.

Since delinquency areas match closely areas considered by the Plowden (1967) and Halsey (1972) Reports as needing 'positive discrimination' in terms of educational resources, the low educational attainments of delinquents is perhaps not surprising. West and Farrington (1977) confirmed this in their recent study. Rutter, Tizard and Whitmore (1970) also demonstrated a close association between low reading attainment and anti-social behaviour in their Isle of Wight study.

In recent years there has been increasing interest expressed in schools as institutions that may help to control delinquency. Both Power et al. (1972) and Gath et al. (1975) found considerable differences in delinquency rates based on schools, which they considered could not be explained by neighbourhood conditions. Hargreaves et

al. (1975) have illustrated the importance of teacher–pupil relationships in relation to deviancy in schools. Truancy has long been related
to delinquency and recently 'unjustified absence' has been the subject
of much attention and some research (e.g. HMSO, 1977b; Galloway,
1976) supplementing the earlier work by Hersov (1960) and Tyerman
(1968) on the causes of school refusal.

There have been many attempts to classify delinquents in terms
of their personality traits (e.g. Quay, 1964). Hewitt and Jenkins
(1946) distinguished three types of delinquents – the neurotic or
overinhibited, the socialized delinquent conforming to his surround-
ings, and the unsocialized aggressive delinquent. The difficulty with
such forms of classification is that too many delinquents appear to
be of a 'mixed' type, not belonging to any particular category (Field,
1967).

Eysenck's personality theory has also been applied to criminal
behaviour (Eysenck, 1964). Feldman (1977) summarizes the theory
and the personality measures derived from it. Briefly, it suggests that
delinquents are more likely to be extravert, neurotic or unstable as
well as high on 'psychotism'. 'Psychotism', as measured by Eysenck's
test, seems to approximate closely to psychopathic qualities, such as
indifference to others and lack of feeling. Passingham (1972) considers
the empirical backing for the theory inadequate and neither Little
(1963), Hoghughi and Forrest (1970) nor West and Farrington (1973)
find much empirical support for it. The importance of situational
factors influencing test responses is stressed by Feldman. Undetected
delinquents enjoying their freedom may not respond (in terms of
extraversion and neuroticism, etc.) in the same way as those who have
been convicted and sent to an institution. This is an area of research
requiring more extensive exploration.

Burt (1925) stressed the importance of high 'emotionality' or
general instability. It is of interest to note that Eysenck has also
emphasized this aspect of delinquent behaviour. He considered the
impulsiveness rather than the sociability component of the extraversion factor as probably more relevant to criminal behaviour
(Eysenck and Eysenck, 1963). It is possible, of course, that it is the
impulsive delinquents who are more often arrested! 'Q scores' (a
measure of impulsiveness) on the long established Porteus Maze Test
still distinguish delinquents from non-delinquents as well as the
recidivist from the less delinquent (Riddle and Roberts, 1977). The
relationship of neurotic conflict to delinquency does not appear strong

(Burt, 1925; Glueck and Glueck, 1950). However, Stott's work (1960, 1977) might suggest otherwise, since he appears to equate his own measure of 'maladjustment' with the existence of 'emotional conflict'.

The psychopathic delinquent or criminal has been the subject of much research (Hare, 1970; Trasler, 1973) but there is controversy over the use of the term (Feldman, 1977). Davies and Maliphant (1971a; 1971b; 1974) have explored the possible extension of psychopathic types of behaviour in the normal school population. This was confirmed in terms of test scores, avoidance learning, and autonomic activity as measured by heart rate, under induced stress and normal conditions. Subsequently, Wadsworth (1976) analysed data on pulse rates of a large sample of children, including delinquents, taken by medical officers in 1957. West and Farrington (1977) also made use of pulse rate data. The findings of both pieces of research gave modest support (West, 1977) to the previous experimental work of Davies and Maliphant in spite of the fact that controls in these studies would unavoidably have been less refined.

Twin studies and chromosomal anomalies, particularly the XYY syndrome, have been the subject of some investigation (Slater et al., 1969; Kahn et al., 1976; Dalgard and Kringlen, 1976). However, although some abnormalities have been discovered in some delinquents, the numbers are so small as to offer little of general explanatory value.

Treatment and prevention

The assumption is usually made that delinquents, having been identified, need 'treatment'. The term raises issues about the nature and aetiology of delinquency briefly considered in the concluding section. In reality, of course, the term 'treatment' needs the widest interpretation for it may cover any form of service, from individual psychotherapy to support for the child's family.

The effectiveness of intervention programmes for delinquents has been seriously questioned both in this country and the United States (e.g. Cornish and Clarke, 1975; Rutherford, 1977; McCord, 1978). While research in this area is notoriously difficult to conduct (Clarke and Cornish, 1972), the indications are that whatever the regime, failure rates in general (as measured by the crude but nevertheless pertinent index-reconviction rates) are high (60–80 per cent over two years). Gibbens (1977) in his review of treatment, however, does indicate some successful programmes. Possible explanations for this regrettable state of affairs are many – such as a poor match between the individual delinquent's personality and 'treatment', difficulties on discharge from the institution, and the crudity of measures of 'deterioration' or 'improvement'. Some residential provision will always be required for some children irrespective of its efficacy but the objectives of the 1969 Act to develop a more comprehensive service within the community would seem amply justified. Conflicts arising from the Act, related to issues of 'care' or 'custody', should be capable of better resolution (Tutt, 1974). The needs of the individual child and of society are surely not incompatible. The fact that, even with the fuller recognition of individual differences between delinquents, the best single predictor of future delinquency is past delinquency, whatever is done in the present, permits no complacency (see Tutt 1978 for a consideration of alternative strategies).

Two forms of treatment for individuals which have developed in recent years are the use of modelling procedures (Sarason, 1971) and, of course, behaviour modification techniques (Davidson and Seidman, 1974; Feldman, 1977). However, more extensive studies are still required with adequate attention paid to controls, pre-treatment base-line measures and longer follow-up periods, to check both on how far the change in behaviour generalizes and also on the extent to which it is maintained in real life situations.

It has been asserted (Beccaria, 1764) that crimes are more effectively prevented by the certainty of punishment rather than its severity. An increase in the probability of detection would appear highly desirable but to achieve this would require a greater involvement of the public and not just increased dependence on an enlarged police force. This may not be so easily achieved. The lack of appropriate action by onlookers to some emergency situations, such as the senseless destruction of property or a vicious attack on an individual, has been the subject of much public comment. However commonsense assertions about the 'indifference' or 'apathy' on the part of the onlookers would not appear to be a sufficient explanation of such situations from the limited research that is available (e.g., Latané and Darley, 1968; Darley and Latané, 1968). Personality variables appear to have little relevance; individuals were concerned about 'victims' even although they took no action to alleviate their distress. Confusion about responsibility for initiating appropriate action seemed to be an important factor, particularly when there were several bystanders present. More explicit and widespread instructions to members of the public on what to do in emergencies might help to elicit more appropriate action by individuals and so reduce crime.

Another approach to reducing crime is of course to restrict opportunities. Open display of goods in shops and supermarkets are an obvious attraction to steal for many, even when they have the means for purchase, as frequent press reports indicate. Mayhew et al. (1976) describe examples where restricting opportunities had a significant effect; one study related to car theft and the other to damage on buses. Car theft was much reduced when steering locks were fitted to new cars in this country, although older cars without steering locks were more at risk as a result. In Germany, the fitting of steering locks was compulsory for all cars irrespective of age and the 'displacement' risk to older cars did not arise. Damage inside buses was found to be related to the degree of supervision of passengers possible by the driver or conductor. Areas more visible to observation received less damage. Such studies usefully draw attention to the importance of situational factors as determined by physical design as well as by the more social and personal element of supervision.

Conclusions

In retrospect, it is difficult to comprehend why it was ever hoped that a general theory or explanation of delinquency could ever be formulated. Delinquents are not a homogeneous group.

Traditionally, and partly under the influence of the medical disease model which assumes a morbid aetiology, the psychological approach to delinquency has tended to encapsulate the principal causes within the individual and his family, on the basis of associations with variables reflecting adversity or abnormality. Until recently little regard was paid to situational determinants. While delinquents may well experience more adversity than others, few of them would claim that they are entirely victims of circumstances rather than agents of their own action. Nevertheless, there is likely to be a disproportionate number of delinquents (but still a minority) who will need specialized help with their personal adjustment problems.

Sociology has produced many interesting theories about delinquency although more empirical backing is still required. The reasons why some and not others become delinquent or recidivists remains unsolved by both the disciplines of psychology and sociology. The appeal of 'labelling theory' (described in Hargreaves et al., 1975; Taylor et al., 1973) is considerable but seems to assume a passivity and lack of initiative amongst delinquents which experience denies (Parker, 1974). Furthermore, in common with other global theories of delinquency, it also has difficulty in explaining the 'spontaneous remission' rates of delinquents, whatever the treatment offered, as well as the general decrement of delinquency with age (Hirschi, 1975). The assertion that it is law that 'criminalizes' behaviour is tenable but law does require a society to establish it. It would also be naive to assume that the removal of law would result in the absence of behaviour which over time has been outlawed by most societies (Walker, 1977).

There is an issue, reflected in the 1969 Act and its critics, which relates to whether the courts should be concerned with what the delinquent *does* or with what he *is*. There would seem to be a tendency in the United States (Rutherford, 1977), possibly as a result of the increase in delinquency coupled with the disappointing results of intervention (McCord, 1978), to press for more limited objectives with an emphasis on 'accountability', both from the delinquents who commit serious crime and from all involved in the judicial process.

References

Andry, R. G. (1960) *Delinquency and Parental Pathology*. London: Methuen.

Baldwin, J. (1975) British areal studies of crime: an assessment. *British Journal of Criminology 15* (3): 211–26.

Banks, C. (1964) *Delinquency and Crime*. Paper given at Keele University for the British Psychological Society.

Beccaria (1764) Essay on crime and punishment. Quoted by L. T. Wilkins (1969) *Evaluation of Penal Measures*. New York: Random House.

Belson, W. A. (1975) *Juvenile Theft: The Causal Factors*. London: Harper and Row.

Bowlby, J. (1946) *Forty-Four Juvenile Thieves*. London: Bailliere, Tindall and Cox.

Bowlby, J., Ainsworth, M., Boston, N. and Rosenbluth, D. (1956) The effects of mother–child separation: a follow-up study. *British Journal of Medical Psychology 29*: 211–47.

Burt, C. (1925) *The Young Delinquent*. London University Press.

Campbell, A. (1977) What makes a girl turn to crime? *New Society*, January 22.

Castle, I. M. and Gittus, E. (1957) The distribution of social defects in Liverpool. *Sociological Review 5*: 43–64.

Christie, N. (1968) Hidden delinquency: some Scandinavian experiences. Paper given at the Cambridge Institute of Criminology, quoted in Hood and Sparks (1970) *Key Issues in Criminology*. London: Weidenfeld and Nicolson.

Christie, N., Andenaes, J. and Skirbekk, S. (1965) A study of self-reported crime. In K. D. Christiansen (ed.) *Scandinavian Studies in Criminology*. London: Tavistock.

Clarke, R. V. G. and Cornish, D. B. (1972) *The Controlled Trial in Institutional Research: Paradigm or Pitfall for Penal Evaluators?* Home Office Research Study, No. 15. London: HMSO.

Cornish, D. B. and Clarke, R. V. G. (1975) *Residential Treatment and its Effects on Delinquency*. Home Office Research Study, No. 32. London: HMSO.

Cowie, J., Cowie, V. and Slater, E. (1968) *Delinquency in Girls*. London: Heinemann.

Dalgard, O. S. and Kringlen, E. (1976) A Norwegian twin study of criminality. *British Journal of Criminology 16* (3): 213–32.

Darley, J. M. and Latané, B. (1968) Bystander interventions in emergencies: diffusion of responsibility. *Journal of Personality and Social Psychology 8*: 377–83.

Davidson, W. S. and Seidman, E. (1974) Studies of behaviour modification and juvenile delinquency. *Psychological Bulletin 81* (12): 998–1011.

Davies, J. G. V. and Maliphant, R. (1971a) Autonomic responses of male adolescents exhibiting refractory behaviour in school. *Journal of Child Psychology and Psychiatry 12*: 115–27.

Davies, J. G. V. and Maliphant, R. (1971b) Refractory behaviour in school in normal adolescent males in relation to psychopathy and early experience. *Journal of Child Psychology and Psychiatry 12*: 35–41.

Davies, J. G. V. and Maliphant, R. (1974) Refractory behaviour in school and avoidance learning. *Journal of Child Psychology and Psychiatry 15*: 23–31.

Douglas, J. W. B., Ross, J. M., Hammon, W. A. and Mulligan, D. G. (1966) Delinquency and social class. *British Journal of Criminology 6*: 294–302.

Eysenck, H. J. (1964) *Crime and Personality*. London: Routledge and Kegan Paul.

Eysenck, H. J. and Eysenck, S. B. G. (1963) On the dual nature of extraversion. *British Journal of Social and Clinical Psychology 2*: 46.

Feldman, M. P. (1977) *Criminal Behaviour: A Psychological Analysis*. Chichester: Wiley.

Field, E. (1967) *A Validation of Hewitt and Jenkins' Hypothesis*. Home Office Research Study, No. 10. London: HMSO.

Ford, D. (1975) *Children, Courts and Caring*. London: Constable.

Galloway, D. (1976) Size of school, socio-economic hardship, suspension rates and persistent unjustified absence from school. *British Journal of Educational Psychology 46* (1): 40–7.

Gath, D., Cooper, B., Gattoni, F. and Rockett, D. (1975) *Child Guidance and Delinquency in a London Borough*. Institute of Psychiatry, Maudsley Monographs, No. 24. Oxford University Press.

Gibbens, T. (1977) Treatment of delinquents. In M. Rutter and L. Hersov (eds) *Child Psychiatry: Modern Approaches*. London: Blackwell Scientific Publications.

Gibbens, T. and Ahrenfeldt, R. H. (1966) *Cultural Factors in Delinquency*. London: Tavistock.

Gibbons, D. (1965) *Changing the Lawbreaker*. Englewood Cliffs, New Jersey: Prentice-Hall.

Glueck, S. and Glueck, E. (1950) *Unravelling Delinquency*. Oxford University Press.

Glueck, S. and Glueck, E. (1960) *Predicting Delinquency and Crime*. Boston: Harvard University Press.

Glueck, S. and Glueck, E. (1969) *Delinquents and Non-Delinquents in Perspective*. Oxford University Press.

Gold, M. (1966) Undetected delinquent behaviour. *Journal of Research in Crime and Delinquency 3*: 27–46.

Goodman, N., Maloney, E., Davies, J., Durkin, P. and Halton, J. (1976) *Further Studies of Female Offenders*. Home Office Research Study, No. 33. London: HMSO.

Halsey, A. H. (1972) *Educational Priority*, Vol. 1. London: HMSO.

Hare, R. D. (1970) *Psychopathy: Theory and Research*. New York: Wiley.

Hargreaves, H. D., Hester, S. K. and Mellor, F. J. (1975) *Deviance in Classrooms*. London: Routledge and Kegan Paul.

HMSO (1963) *The Children and Young Persons Act*. London: HMSO.

HMSO (1965) *The Child, the Family and the Young Offender*. London: HMSO.

HMSO (1968a) *Children in Trouble*. London: HMSO.

HMSO (1968b) *Social Work Scotland Act*. London: HMSO.

HMSO (1968c) *Report of the Committee on Local Authority and Allied Social Services. The Seebohm Report*. London: HMSO.

HMSO (1969) *The Children and Young Persons Act*. London: HMSO.

HMSO (1970) *The Local Authority Social Services Act*. London: HMSO.

HMSO (1972) *The Local Government Act*. London: HMSO.

HMSO (1975a) *Eleventh Report from the House of Commons Expenditure Committee: The Children and Young Persons Act*, 1. London: HMSO.

HMSO (1975b) *The Children Act*. London: HMSO.

HMSO (1977a) *Criminal Statistics: England and Wales, 1976*. London: HMSO.

HMSO (1977b) *The Pack Report: Truancy and Indiscipline in Schools in Scotland*. Scottish Education Department. London: HMSO.

Hersov, L. A. (1960) Persistent non-attendance at school. *Journal of Child Psychology and Psychiatry 1*: 130–6.

Hewitt, L. and Jenkins, R. (1946) *Fundamental Patterns of Maladjustment: The Dynamics of their Origin*. Springfield, Illinois: State Printer.

Hirschi, S. (1969) *Causes of Delinquency*. University of California Press.

Hirschi, T. (1975) Labelling theory and juvenile delinquency: an assessment of the evidence. In W. R. Gove (ed.) *The Labelling of Deviance: Evaluating a Perspective*. New York: Sage Publications.

Hirschi, T. and Selvin, H. C. (1967) *Delinquency Research: An Appraisal of Analytic Methods*. New York: The Free Press.

Hoghughi, M. S. and Forrest, A. R. (1970) Eysenck's theory of criminality: an examination with approved school boys. *British Journal of Criminology 10*: 240–54.

Hood, R. and Sparks, R. (1970) *Key Issues in Criminology*. London: Weidenfeld and Nicolson.

Inkeles, A. (1961) Personality and social structure. In R. K. Merton (ed.) *Sociology Today: Problems and Prospects*. New York: Basic Books.

Jones, H. (1965) *Crime in a Changing Society*. London: Penguin Books.

Kahn, J., Reed, F. S., Bates, M., Coates, T. and Everitt, B. (1976) A survey of Y chromosome variants and personality in 436 Borstal lads and 254 controls. *British Journal of Criminology 16* (3): 233–44.

Lander, B. (1954) *Towards an Understanding of Delinquency*. New York: Columbia University Press.

Latané, B. and Darley, J. M. (1968) Group inhibition of bystanders intervention in emergencies. *Journal of Personality and Social Psychology 10*: 215–21.

Little, A. (1963) Professor Eysenck's theory of crime: an empirical test on adolescent young offenders. *British Journal of Criminology 4*: 152–63.

McCord, J. (1978) A thirty-year follow-up of treatment effects. *American Psychologist 33* (3): 284–9.

McCord, W., McCord, J. and Zola, I. K. (1959) *Origins of Crime: A New Evaluation of the Cambridge-Somerville Youth Study*. New York: Columbia University Press.

McDonald, L. (1969) *Social Class and Delinquency*. London: Faber and Faber.

Maliphant, R. (1972) *Recidivism: Ecological Factors, Parent–Child Relations and Some Personality Attributes*. University of London, doctoral thesis.

Manning, P. K. (1975) Deviance and dogma. *British Journal of Criminology 15* (1): 1–20.

Mayhew, P., Clarke, R. V. G., Sturman, A. and Hough, H. M. (1976) *Crime as Opportunity*. Home Office Research Study, No. 34. London: HMSO.

Morris, T. (1957) *The Criminal Area: A Study in Social Ecology*. London: Routledge and Kegan Paul.

O'Hagan, F. J. (1976) Gang characteristics: an empirical survey. *Journal of Child Psychology and Psychiatry 17* (4): 305–14.

Parker, H. J. (1974) *View from the Boys*. Newton Abbot: David and Charles.

Passingham, R. E. (1972) Crime and personality: a review of Eysenck's theory. In V. D. Nebylitsyn and J. A. Gray (eds) *Biological Bases of Individual Behaviour*. London: Academic Press.

Plowden Report (1967) *Children and their Primary Schools*. Vols 1 and 2. London: HMSO.

Power, M. J. (1966) Personal communication.

Power, M. J., Benn, R. T. and Morris, J. N. (1972) Neighbourhood, school and juveniles before the courts. *British Journal of Criminology 12*: 111–32.

Quay, H. (1964) Dimension of personality in delinquent boys as inferred from the factor analysis of case history data. *Child Development 35*: 479–84.

Radzinowicz, L. (1964) The criminal in society. *Journal of the Royal Society of Arts 112*: 916–29.

Riddle, M. and Roberts, A. H. (1977) Delinquency, delay of gratification, recidivism, and the Porteus Maze Tests. *Psychological Bulletin 84* (3): 417–25.

Robinson, W. S. (1950) Ecological correlations and the behaviour o
individuals. *American Sociological Review 15*: 351–7.

Rutherford, A. (1977) *Youth Crime Policy in the United States*. Croydon
Institute for the Study and Treatment of Delinquency.

Rutter, M. L. (1971) Parent–child separation: psychological effects on the
children. *Journal of Child Psychology and Psychiatry 12*: 233–60.

Rutter, M. L. and Madge, N. (1976) *Cycles of Disadvantage*. London
Heinemann.

Rutter, M. L., Tizard, J. and Whitmore, K. (1970) *Education, Health an
Behaviour*. London: Longmans.

Sarason, I. G. (1971) *Modeling: An Approach to the Rehabilitation of Juvenil
Offenders*. Research Report, University of Washington.

Schmid, C. F. (1960) Urban crime areas. *American Sociological Review 25*
527–42 and 655–78.

Sellin, T. and Wolfgang, M. E. (1964) *The Measurement of Delinquency*. London
Wiley.

Shaw, C. R. and McKay, H. D. (1932) Are broken homes a causative facto
in juvenile delinquency? *Social Forces 10*: 514–24.

Shaw, C. R. and McKay, H. D. (1942, rev. 1969) *Juvenile and Delinquency
Areas*. Chicago University Press.

Simon, F. H. (1971) *Prediction Methods in Criminology*. Home Office Research
Study, No. 7. London: HMSO.

Slater, E. T. O., Kahn, J., Carter, W. I. and Dernley, N. (1969) Chromosome
studies in remand home and prison populations. In D. J. West (ed.)
Criminological Implications of Chromosome Abnormalities. Cambridge: Institute o
Criminology.

Stott, D. H. (1960) Delinquency, maladjustment and unfavourable ecology
British Journal of Psychology 51 (2): 157–70.

Stott, D. H. and Wilson, D. N. (1977) The adult criminal as juvenile
British Journal of Criminology 17 (1): 47–57.

Tappan, P. W. (1947) Who is the criminal? *American Sociological Review 12*
96–102.

Taylor, I., Walton, P. and Young, J. (1973) *The New Criminology: For a
Social Theory of Deviance*. London: Routledge and Kegan Paul.

Taylor, L., Morris, A. and Downes, D. (1976) *Signs of Trouble*. London
British Broadcasting Corporation.

Tennent, G. and Gath, D. (1975) Bright delinquents. *British Journal o
Criminology 15* (4): 386–90.

Trasler, G. (1973) Criminal behaviour. In H. J. Eysenck (ed.) *Handbook o
Abnormal Psychology*. London: Pitman Medical.

Tutt, N. S. (1974) *Care or Custody*. London: Longman and Todd.

Tutt, N. S. (ed.) (1978) *Alternative Strategies for Coping with Crime*. Oxford and
London: Blackwell and Robertson.

Tyerman, M. J. (1968) *Truancy*. London: University of London Press.

US Government (1967) *The Present's Commission on Law Enforcement and
Administration of Justice*. Washington: US Government Printing Office.

US Government (1974) *The Juvenile Justice and Delinquency Prevention Act*
Washington: US Government Printing Office.

Wadsworth, M. E. J. (1976) Delinquency, pulse rates and early emotional deprivation. *British Journal of Criminology 16* (3): 245–56.

Walker, N. (1977) *Behaviour and Misbehaviour: Explanations and Non-Explanations.* Oxford: Blackwell.

Wallis, C. P. and Maliphant, R. (1967) Delinquent areas in the county of London: ecological factors. *British Journal of Criminology 7* (3): 250–84.

Walters, A. A. (1956) A note on statistical methods of predicting delinquency. *British Journal of Delinquency 6* (4).

West, D. J. (1967) *The Young Offender.* London: Penguin Books.

West, D. J. (1977) Delinquency. In M. Rutter and L. Hersov (eds) *Child Psychiatry: Modern Approaches.* Oxford: Basil Blackwell.

West, D. J. and Farrington, D. P. (1973) *Who Becomes Delinquent?* London: Heinemann.

West, D. J. and Farrington, D. P. (1977) *The Delinquent Way of Life.* London: Heinemann.

Wilkins, L. T. (1966) *Evaluation of Penal Measures.* New York: Random House.

Wolfgang, M. E., Figlio, R. N. and Sellin, T. (1972) *Delinquency in a Birth Cohort.* University of Chicago Press.

Woodward, M. (1955) The role of low intelligence in delinquency. *British Journal of Delinquency 5* (4): 281–303.

Wootton, B. (1959) *Social Science and Social Pathology.* London: Allen and Unwin.

Name index

Prosser, H., 135, *143*
Pugh, G., 134, *142*
Puka, W., 50, *77*

Quay, H., 160, *167*

Radin, N., *143*
Radzinowicz, L., 145, 151, *167*
Rau, L., *77*
Rawls, J., 50, *77*
Reed, F. S., *167*
Rest, J. R., 56, *77*
Reynolds, D., 139, 140, *142*
Riddle, M., 160, *167*
Riesman, D., 103, *120*
Rinkskopf, D., 138, *142*
Roberts, A. H., 160, *167*
Robinson, M. Z., *44*
Robinson, W. S., 156, *168*
Rockett, D., *165*
Rodgon, M. M., 35, *44*
Roff, M., 114, 115, *120*
Rosenberg, F., *23, 45*
Rosenberg, M., 8, 18, *23, 45*
Rosenblum, L., 101, 113, *119*
Rosenbluth, D., *164*
Rosenhan, D. L., 65, *77*
Rosenthal, R., 25, *45*
Ross, J., *141*
Ross, J. M., *165*
Rotter, J. B., 25, *45*
Rousseau, J. J., 52, *77*
Rubin, K. H., 35, *45*
Rutherford, A., 161, 164, *168*
Rutherford, J., 101, *119*
Rutter, M., 12–13, 15, *23*, 133, 139, *143*,
   152, 158, 159, *168*

Salmon, P., 114, *120*
Salzstein, H. D., 68, *75*
Sanford, N., 85, 92, *94*
Sanford, R. N., *73*
Sarason, I. G., 162, *168*
Schmid, C. F., 154, *168*
Schofield, M., 112, *120*
Schwartz, S., 66, *77*
Sears, R. R., 36, *45*, 53, *77*
Seglow, J., 134, *143*
Seidman, E., 162, *165*
Sellin, T., 153, *168, 169*
Selman, R. L., 35, *45*, 59–60, *77*
Selvin, H. C., 153, 157, *166*
Sharma, S., 38, *45*

Shaw, C. R., 154, 155, 156, 157, *168*
Sherif, C., 98, 99, 100, 107, *120*
Sherif, M., 98, 99, 100, 107, *120*
Shinman, S., 138, *143*
Simmons, R., 16, 17, *23*
Simon, F. H., 153, *168*
Simon, W., 80, *93*
Simpson, H. R., *141*
Skinner, B. F., 49–50, *78*
Skirbekk, S., *165*
Slater, E. T. O., 161, *165, 168*
Smith, A. J., 100, *120*
Smith, M. B., 58, *75*
Solomon, R. L., 54, *78*
Sparks, R., 144, 145, 146, 149, *167*
Speicher-Dubin, B., *76*
Speier, M., 117, *120*
Spence, J., 80, 92, *94*
Stanford Research Institute, 137, *143*
Stone, L. J., 38, *45*
Stott, D. H. 156, 161, *168*
Stroud, J., 73, *75*
Stubbs, M., 99, *120*
Sturman, A., *167*
Sturt, R., 102, *120*
Sugarman, B., 70, *78*
Sullivan, E. V., 30, *43*, 61, *78*
Sullivan, H. S., 110, *120*
Swainson, B. M., 63, *78*
Swanson, G. E., 103, *120*
Swift, B., 105, *119*
Symonds, P. M., 85, *94*
Synnerdale, V., 38, *44*

Taba, H., 63, *75*
Tappan, P. W., 154, *168*
Taylor, I., 144, 147, 148, 164, *168*
Tennent, G., 159, *168*
Terman, L., 80, 83, *94*
Thornton, D., 58, *78*
Thrasher, F. M., 100, 108, *120*
Tizard, B., 134, *143*
Tizard, J., 159, *168*
Toder, N. L., 42, *45*
Tomé, H. R., 17, *23*
Trainer, F. E., 61, *78*
Trasler, G., 161, *168*
Tucker, M., 92, *94*
Tulkin, S. R., 31, *45*
Turiel, E., 56, *77, 78*
Turner, L. H., *78*
Tutt, N. S., 162, *168*
Tyerman, M. J., 160, *168*

176   The School Years

Subject index